Oliver's Towns

With dear wishes —
Gary Hiebert
(Oliver Towne)

Oliver's Towns

More Columns by Oliver Towne

by Gareth Hiebert

ISBN 1-880654-19-9

Library of Congress Card Number 00-102779

Permission from Walker Lundy, Editor, to reprint articles
contained in the St. Paul Dispatch and St. Paul
Pioneer Press is gratefully acknowledged.

Pre-press by North Star Press of St. Cloud, Inc.

Published by
Pogo Press, Incorporated
Four Cardinal Lane
St. Paul, Minnesota 55127

OTHER BOOKS BY GARETH HIEBERT

The Man on the Street Visits a St. Paul Public School. St. Paul, Minnesota: St. Paul Dispatch and Pioneer Press, 1958.

Saint Paul is my beat. St. Paul, Minnesota: The North Central Publishing Company, 1958.

Once Upon a Towne. St. Paul, Minnesota: The North Central Publishing Company, 1959.

Oliver's Travels. St. Paul, Minnesota: The North Central Publishing Company, 1973.

A Dream Comes True. Memories of Mantorville. Mantorville, Minnesota: I. Pappas, 1978.

My Years at St. Olaf. From Melby to Mel. Northfield, Minnesota: St. Olaf College, 1988.

Little Canada, a Voyageur's Vision: History of Little Canada. Stillwater, Minnesota: Croixside Press, 1989.

The Dacotah History Hotel. 1859 to 1972. New Ulm, Minnesota: New Ulm Graphics, 1989.

Fragments. The Art of Lloyd Herfindahl. Lake Mills, Iowa: Stoyles Graphic Services, 1994.

City on Seven Hills. Columns of Oliver Towne. St. Paul, Minnesota: Pogo Press, Incorporated, 1999.

Preface

This is a collection of travel stories and other adventures. It is for armchair travelers who wish to visit or revisit the far-flung reaches of Europe from home. It is also about interesting Minnesota people and places closer to home.

These adventures began in August of 1945 in Lucerne, Switzerland. I was a soldier waiting to come home and got a week's tour of Switzerland to pass the time.

That taste of travel was savored and I vowed to return.

I did. With my wife. On Easter Monday of 1964, Janet and I boarded the French liner "France" (now "Norway") at Pier 84 in New York City for a magic carpet trip of five weeks in Europe. It was one of the last European crossings that ship made. It was luxurious, romantic and unforgettable. For us it was an incredible beginning.

Who knew then that this would lead to 28 more trips to Europe?

But it did. The trip was infectious. Janet fell in love with Paris and all of France and that love affair never diminished. But we had equally warm feelings about Denmark, Bavaria, Italy, Spain, Greece, and Turkey.

In 28 years we worshipped with two popes, spent New Year's Eve in the mountains of Bavaria, crossed Checkpoint Charlie twice when the Iron Curtain was still up, sailed down the Danube to Communist Budapest, Hungary. Adventures!

One Sunday we ate lunch with Julia Child in her French home in Southern France.

I was made a Chevalier (knight) of the Bordeaux Vendange (Bordeaux wine festival.)

We spent two weeks living in a series of Rhine River castles.

Janet and I looked for the Loch Ness monster in Scotland and never found it, but enjoyed meeting a delightful hotel barmaid named Fiona.

We spent an afternoon with artist Salvador Dali in his Spanish home by the sea and shared a huge hotel at the top of the 10,000 foot Zugspitze in Bavaria with two charming German bus hostesses — all four of us and one mouse.

In 1968 we took our four children to Rome for Christmas and saw Pope Paul VI on Christmas morning in St. Peter's.

We had some unexpected adventures. Once, enroute to Europe, one of the passengers gave birth to a baby at 33,000 feet over the North Atlantic. That changed the course of the trip and we had to land in Newfoundland so she and the baby could be taken to a hospital and the plane with the rest of us finally took off again for Frankfurt, Germany. I sat in a hotel smoking room and wrote a story about this unexpected Christmas present on TWA flight 740 and got a $50 bonus.

One afternoon in Greece, my wife and I ran the course in the Olympia stadium, where the first Olympics were held.

In 1996 we left Europe for the last time and as the United Airlines plane swept into the air off Charles de Gaulle airport in Paris, we looked down on the city that was our second home.

The last time we saw Paris, it was a beautiful sight. Janet never saw it again.

But here you will enjoy Europe. You will also like stories of our visits to St. Paul and to other places in outstate Minnesota. These are tales of Oliver's towns. You will find, I am sure, that towns everywhere are filled with wonderful stories just waiting for the visitor to discover.

Gareth Hiebert
St. Paul, Minnesota
April 24, 2000

DEDICATION

This book is dedicated to our four children
—Julie, Polly, James and Daniel—
who shared many of these travels with us.

CONTENTS

My Town and Yours

New Ulm was my first town. After college and the Army St.
Paul became my home, as it still is, serving as the source and
inspiration for what Oliver Towne would write as the fol-
lowing column indicates.

Writer keeps finding topics all over town

"This column will be mainly about towns—yours and mine!"

That was the first sentence of the first Oliver Towne column, which appeared Nov. 1, 1954.

Today begins the 30th year.

And I thought that you might like to read that first Oliver Towne over my shoulder today:

"In the beginning," I wrote that day, "we'll write mostly about my town, because it will take time to understand yours.

"Viewed from a distance, my town is a pyramiding, jagged line of buildings—red brick, gray, salmon-colored, streaked by weather and smudged from smoke and grit.

"By day, the panes of thousands of windows reflect the sun and by night gleam as pinpoints of light that go out one by one, as if touched by an unseen hand, until the skyline is only a dark hulk in the moonlight.

"Close up, the city is lines of cars, darting in and out of threading traffic; it is the people who pour out of the buildings at noonday, who form a glut of humanity at Seventh and Wabasha, who

1

jostle each other amid a rustle of packages on the buses that weave out of the Loop at 5 p.m.

"The city is the cop on the beat at Ninth and Wabasha at 1 a.m., the children crawling over the slides and swings on a school playground in the sunshine of a warm, spring day.

"It is the lonely switchmen in the railroad yards, talking their own language with lanterns, and it is the rising moan of the siren from the ambulance, the fire engine or police car.

"The city is the smoky convention hall and the slam-bang music from a dance hall on West Seventh on Saturday night where a bride and groom dash out to their car amid a shower of rice and cheers.

"My town is the magnificent swell of a church choir's hymn on Sunday morning.

"This town is a blend of the old and new, both in people and architecture. The quicksand of the rollicking river town it was more than a century ago had solidified into a firm foundation of grace and poise.

"Out of all this has come a personality called St. Paul.

"But essentially, doesn't this describe something of your town, too?

"Nestling along the rivers, rising off the plains and out of the pine forests—with water tower, church steeple or smokestack pointing the way down U.S. 14, 212, 12, 61?

"You are now entering Brainerd, Cloquet, Duluth, North-field, New Ulm, Mankato, Nicollet, Springfield, Hudson.

"Population 100,000, 1,000, 2,000, 10,000.

"Speed limit 30 miles an hour. Drive safely and save our children.

"Street lights, cars, people, taverns, schools, churches, whining sirens, plaintive train whistles, boisterous Friday nights or Monday nights on Main Street.

"We will write about these things, examining the byways, the crannies; touching here on history, there on the future, but more often on the present. We will try to put together little by little the pieces of the puzzle called 'any' town."

And I have kept that promise in millions of words and thousands of miles traveled, most of them in this city, which is My Town.

The city I knew then exists only in fragments. Old neighborhoods are gone—the West Side Flats, the old 13th Street Neighborhood, the Italian Upper Levee, Swede Hollow, old Central Park place below the capitol. I roamed and wrote about them all.

The new has risen out of the rubble. But the charm of the past is still there in Rice Park, Landmark Center, the Cathedral, the Summit Avenue mansions, the Pioneer Building, Market House and Mears Park.

It is brown bagging it on a bench near the splashing Irvine Park fountain and browsing the cul de sacs on Summit-Hill. Most of all, it is writing about the people. A long procession of people, big and small, picturesque and famous and some infamous, have marched across the written stage of Oliver Towne and disappeared into the wings. Now, I write about their children and children's children.

Many were my friends. I miss them. Sometimes when I walk the city streets at night I see their faces again in the mist of the past.

I remember the late Lois Hatton, fashion writer, telling me that November day in 1954, "I don't envy you. Have you ever thought of the millions of words you'll have to write?"

I never have; I've enjoyed writing all of them.
(November 1, 1983.)

Lunch with Julia Child

Touch me, ladies! I had lunch with Julia Child one noon last week.

Sat at her right, I did, sharing a nibble of her sweet potato pie and nice bites of her chocolate Victoire.

"Come on, have another bite," she said, as we crossed forks together in Winfield Potter's St. Anthony Main saloon and restaurant.

What does the world's high priestess of French cuisine eat when she's not doing her own cooking or writing about it?

Barbecued ribs, sweet potato pie and a big side of goodies from the salad bar, coated with ample salad dressings, in this instance.

Our French Chef eats as if she had just spent the morning on a threshing crew instead of appearing on TV and autographing her new and sixth book *Julia Child and more company*, which is why she was in the Twin Cities.

It wasn't the first time I've had lunch with Julia and her husband, Paul, who sat across the round table.

We both remembered one warm and sunny June Sunday in 1972 when my wife and I were invited for dinner with the Childs at their "escape hatch" on a slope near Grasse, in southern France, a salt spray away from the Riviera.

That noon Julia barbecued a goatkin (young goat) for us and served it crusty with a mustard sauce and a ragout of Vegetable Provençal, a composed salad reminiscent of a Salade Niçoise.

She remembered that menu, too, as she licked her fingers from the big slab of barbecued ribs, urging me to sample one.

But I, loyal to the French Chef's gospel, ate a light lunch, sailing through a pineapple hull filled with chunks of chicken salad in walnut dressing, pieces of pineapple and a bunch of chilled, seedless grapes.

"Well, this is a surprise," she repeated as we ate and chatted about what the 1980s hold for us.

"I am the eternal optimist. I think we will all eat better and have a beautiful relationship with food," said she, who revolutionized the art and appreciation of cooking in the 1970s.

"I suppose we have been eating too much meat and expensive cuts and it is time for us to begin to use it all—the way the Europeans do. Yes, I think we are going to begin eating as they do in Europe. Inflation will demand it—and also the wider use of vegetables."

For her part, Julia is focusing on exploration—using unfamiliar vegetables like turnips, collard greens, yellow summer squash, unfamiliar fish like skate, Ocean Pollock, monkfish—"all delicious." She is crusading for things like boiled chicken with garlic and cheese sauce, leek and rabbit pie.

"People say to me, 'Julia, we like fish, but the smell when you're working with it...'"

"I say, if it smells, throw it out. It isn't fresh."

Speaking of throwing, I told her, "One of my readers wanted to tell you that what endears you to her is the nonchalance, the ease with which you work on those TV shows. When you drop a roast or a pot of coq au vin, you just pick it up and go on."

"Hrrrmph," said Julia.

"It's amazing how these stories get around. I think I dropped a head of lettuce once and people have had me dropping stuffed roast geese, whole hams, chickens and dusting them off and putting them back on the cutting board.

"Here," she said, "won't you have one small barbequed rib? They're delicious." (I can see that on the Winfield Potter Menu: "Recommended by Julia Child.")

"You know, if I had a large family to take out, I certainly couldn't afford to take them to a fancy place (like Lutece in New York). I'd take them to some Burger Chef (oops! "Our burgers recommended by Julia Child") or place like it. Don't you think that with so much exposure and conformity, their kitchens have to be neat and clean because of all the inspections?"

She suddenly felt the urge to examine the salad bar and offered to get me a platter of whatever looked good.

I lowered my eyes, demurely, and said, "Non, merci. I always eat like Julia Child in the book."

"Have you been to China?" she said when she returned, heavy laden with greens.

I said I hadn't and didn't have much inclination to go.

By now, as Julia and I were polishing off her wedge of the chocolate Victoire, the kitchen staff of Winfield Potter's had assembled to pay homage to "la reine de la cuisine de tout le monde." (The world's queen of cuisine.)

She knighted them all in words, especially the chef, Tobie Nidetz who, I thought, was going to swoon in ecstacy.

Then it was up, up and away in her long, black limousine to cook at Dayton's and autograph books at B. Dalton.

I know some people who won't buy one, though.

They're the people in the St. Anthony Main shops, especially the food-oriented stores, who waited in vain to shake hands with Julia.

She was willing, but alas, her entourage, which surrounds her like the pastry encasing a beef Wellington, whisked her into the middle distance before she could utter even one "Bon appetit." (March 18, 1980.)

A link to a literary era

I almost missed the brief note in the Dispatch about the passing of Fred Wolfe, brother of author Thomas Wolfe, who wrote *Look Homeward Angel, Of Time and the River,* and *You Can't Go Home Again,* a title which has become a household phrase in the English language.

Fred was the model for the character of Luke Grant in *Look Homeward Angel* and he stuttered.

But Fred had almost lost that stutter in August 1963 when I spent an afternoon in the cool shade of the crepe myrtle trees at his comfortable home in Spartanburg, S.C.

It was as close to that immortal fraternity of this century's great writers and artists as I ever got—that company of Tom Wolfe, F. Scott Fitzgerald, Ernest Hemingway, Sinclair Lewis, James Joyce, Gertrude Stein, Alice B. Toklas, editor Max Perkins.

But I felt very close to all of them that day in Fred Wolfe's house.

I'd been an Army Reserve major commanding a public information, broadcast and writing team out of the U.S. Continental Army Command at Fort Monroe, Va. during my two weeks' annual active duty for training stint. We were on a maneuver called Swift Strike III.

There was a lull in the "war," and I wandered over to the Spartanburg newspaper, introduced myself and wondered if there was anybody in town worth interviewing.

"Well, if you ever read Thomas Wolfe, maybe his brother, Fred, will do," said the city editor.

Fred Wolfe would do just fine. Often, late at night, I take down from my bookshelf something by Thomas Wolfe, whose descriptions of a city and riding through the night on a passenger train are masterpieces.

You can almost hear the whistle of the old steam locomotive and the clickety-clack of the wheels.

So I called Fred Wolfe and he said to come over about 2 p.m. for a late lunch and iced tea.

He looked like Will Rogers. He had the same easy drawl, the same slow smile. Fred was 67 then, just retired from his executive post with Foremost Dairies in Atlanta.

"You said you were an admirer of Tom's writing. I like that. I'm devoting my retirement to giving him his place in the sun and preserving the old Wolfe house as a museum in Asheville, N.C.," Fred said.

Tom, he suggested, should still be alive, except for the pneumonia and lung congestion caused by excesses in living that killed him in 1938 at the age of 38. It was that merry-go-round that Hemingway rode much longer as well as Franklin P. Adams, Dorothy Parker, Bob Benchley, Alexander Woollcott, and Harold Ross of the *New Yorker* magazine. F. Scott Fitzgerald and his wife Zelda rode it not as long.

Fred Wolfe's fierce love for his brother still flamed as he spoke, as he got out photos of the Wolfe home. He showed me the swing on the porch where they all courted, even Tom.

"Zelda Fitzgerald sat on that swing in the last days of her life," said Fred.

"She had come to stay with us. Scott and Tom were in California, writing stories. She had a relapse of her mental illness and we had to take her to the asylum. It burned, and she with it, not long after. I can still see us standing on the lawn in the devilish glow and watching the place go and hearing the screams from inside. And there was nothing we could do."

As Fred spoke, the distance was narrowed between Asheville and Summit Avenue in St. Paul where Scott and Zelda had lived—or Scott had lived—No. 599 Summit and the Commodore Hotel. As I described them, Fred was fascinated.

Tom Wolfe had been in some torment with his writing. His hometown had disowned him, he'd been sued, and he'd grappled with his publishers, his editors.

"It took Tom seven years before he'd come home after his first book, *Look Homeward Angel*," said Fred. "He was afraid of reaction from the townspeople. What he'd done is not ridicule them, but tell a story of fiction—fact with purpose—of people, and he knew these people best. He wove them into the tapestry of the town. They threatened to drag him across the square. But you know, when he finally came home again, those same people were his best friends. He'd made them famous. Tom, they said, you didn't write enough—about the others."

Fred chuckled.

That summer of 1963 Tom Wolfe was in one of his ascendencies of popularity, at the crest of the waves that rose and fell, like the F. Scott Fitzgerald mania of the early 1970s. The same waves affected the reputations of the others—even Hemingway—who belong to a faded lifestyle.

"They all had one thing in common," said Fred. "They knew how to write."

As I left him that afternoon, he handed me a photograph of him and Tom taken July 30, 1937. He signed it and said, "I mightily wish it were Tom's signature and not mine."

Back in the hotel I read, "Every best wish to Gary Hiebert, from Wolfe's unpredictable brother, 'Luke.'"
(April 22, 1980.)

Queens reunite 25th time

"I'll propose a toast," said the 85-year-old former motor-cycle rider-opera singer, sitting at my left.

"To those of us who are here and those who were here (over) the last 25 years," said Lillian Slaby Mayettte.

Six glasses, mostly ice water, were raised with hers.

Other noontime diners in the Summit Room of the Athletic Club peered into the corner at the long table, the words forming silently on their lips: "Who are they?"

"The original queens of the St. Paul Winter Carnival," I called over. "Seven of the more than 30 queens of the 1916-17 Carnival. That year they were all so beautiful, nobody was picked a winner. They all were."

Oliver Towne (Gary Hiebert) was chosen as Prime Minister for the 1962 St. Paul Winter Carnival. Here he appears with the 1962 Queen of the Snows, Penny Hicks Olson, and Minneapolis' 1961 Aquatennial Queen, Judy Mellin Colby, on the left.

None was less than 80-plus, except Natalie Ayers, Miss Business and Professional Women, who is 65 this year. And myself, the only male and mascot of the club.

Twenty-seven turned out for the first Queens Reunion in 1956, summoned by Tillie Seiberlich Manderfeld, Miss 1916 Golden Rule store. She was not present on this 25th reunion, but she called in from Lakeridge Health Center with best wishes.

Parlor B in the club was hardly big enough to accommodate them all those first few years.

Some have never missed. Like Lillian Slaby Mayette, who was Miss 1916 McPherson-Langford motorcycle shop queen.

At my right was Rose Arend Kohler, 88, Miss Hanna Coal of 1916, proud owner of a new car, which she didn't drive that day because of the snow.

She was tied for the age prize with Sigrid Peterson Monson, who came with her twin daughters, Mrs. Judy Carr and Mrs. Jean Carlson. Sigrid was reminiscing about her queenly years as Miss St. Paul *Daily News.* "Did you know Howard Kahn, the publisher, who cleaned up City Hall and had a body guard in those times?"

Mabelle Peltz Pearson, Miss 1916 Brown Studio, missed last year because of a broken leg, but she was agile at 85 with her cane as a helper and eager to report her first great grandchild, a boy,—"maybe a Winter Carnival king some day."

But she couldn't match the record of Marie O'Connell O'Neill, Miss West Publishing of 1917, who ticks off 47 grandchildren, 28 great grandchildren and "three on the shelf."

Just then the 1981 Royal Party swept through the Summit Room and found the original queens. Queen of

Snows Linda Marie Grant's blonde beauty awed those lovelies of 65 years ago. She kissed them all and Olga Kingsly Delaney, 84, Miss Brown & Bigelow of 1917, looked at her daughter-in-law, Rita Delaney and said, wistfully:

"Were we ever that young and pretty?"

"Oh, yes," said Marie O'Neill. "We were all that beautiful, don't you remember?"

And some of them remembered the nights they partied until the wee hours and Louis Hill Sr. entertained them and the dog sled racers in his Summit Avenue mansion with a lavish candlelight buffet. It's all in the big souvenir picture book a few bring.

Natalie Ayers called their attention to some absent members who sent greetings:

Mildred Fuhrman Ormsby, Miss Minnehaha Dry Cleaners of 1917, who is 91 and decided to stay home because of the cold, but "will see you next year."

And Ann Steigauf Laverty, Miss 1916 Bannon's department store, rang in from Wilder Residence to say she was itching to be there, but the itching of shingles kept her home. Esther Schutte Kowalski, Miss 1916 Scheffer & Rossum, checked in by letter because of a broken hip. And so did Marie Westphalinger, Miss Hussars of 1917, who is in Highland Chateau.

"I think," said Natalie, in a toast of ice water, "we have all gracefully worn the wrinkles of our accomplishments and none has outlived the enthusiasm for life."

We all drank to that.

(February 16, 1981.)

Remembering Gentille

The last time I was with Gentille Yarusso, we were having lunch in Geno's Payne Avenue Italian restaurant and he was talking about his favorite subject—the Italian neighborhood along "the Avenue" in the days past.

He toyed with a small ensalata, two meatballs and a glass of chianti as he spun out his feelings and vivid vignettes of almost 70 years along that stretch of Payne from Minnehaha and Hamm's (now Olympia) brewery to E. Seventh Street, with tiny streets fingering like arms in both directions.

Hidden among the neat, tiny houses, were those lush gardens of the Italian "green thumbs" and far below "the Avenue" was Swede Hollow. Old Lincoln School stood like an educational citadel on one hill, where the "greening" of hundreds of Italian boys and girls took place. Not far away at Woodward and Payne, the gray, stucco Christ Child Community Center was where the Americanization of their parents took place.

And over it all hung the aromas of crusty, Italian bread baking in outdoor brick ovens.

This was Gentille (they always called him Gendy) Yarusso's Payne Avenue and he wrote about it with a facile pen and mind, filling files full of tales of the first generation immigrant families. Many of his stories found their way into the pages of these newspapers, neighborhood gazettes, small publications and mimeographed sheets coveted by families about whom he wrote.

He wrote about the little things of life in that time—always so big in memories.

But since a week ago, he will write no more.

The bard, the sage, the historian of "the Avenue" was buried one day last week from St. Ambrose Catholic Church. It wasn't the church named St. Ambrose he often described. That church stood on lower Payne around Collins and is now a warehouse or machine shop or some such prosaic thing.

I met Gentille in 1946 when I was writing about the city's ethnic communities. Everyone referred me to Gendy because even then he was the historian, the oracle of "the Avenue"—working in the Hamm's bottling department by day and studying and writing at night. He finally got his high school diploma, a feat which earned the respect of his teachers for this heavy-set, bespectacled, gentleman.

That noon in Geno's I urged him to talk about his stories and what he saw when he walked "the Avenue."

"I come in here to Geno's," he said, "and sniff the spicy aromas and I go back to the old Italian grocery stores around Payne and Bradley. One could inhale those stores," he said. "The rich, garlicky and pungent odors of pickle brine and cheese, olives and fish overflowing through open windows and store entrances."

Gendy was off into a reverie. I followed eagerly.

In memory, he and I roamed through the back rooms of those stores, tables piled high with rounds of cheese, some weighing 30 and 40 pounds, freshly made sausages hung to dry on long, wooden sticks, crates of baccalau and smelts.

He twisted his wineglass and peered through the clear, purple radiance and we were off again to those Octobers when the harvest of grapes from the backyard arbors was in and the new wine in the vats.

"All fall and winter we waited and then one day father said it was time to test. It was a ritual. Prohibition or no pro- hibition, every Italian family in the neighborhood made wine. Mother would light a candle and lead a prayer that the wine would be good. Then we'd stand and watch father tap the first barrel, taste, roll it around in his mouth, swallow. He wouldn't say a word, but hand a glass to mother. She would repeat the ritual, then say, 'The wine is good. The good Lord has been good to us.'"

Gentille rolled the last drops of Geno's chianti around in his mouth, then looked at his empty glass and smiled, almost sadly.

"I miss those good things. With my diet, one glass is a celebration."

Gentille loved music, especially opera. The love ran in his family. He liked to tell about his Uncle Frank, who was an accomplished musician and singer. Uncle Frank decided one summer to write and produce an opera on Payne Avenue called *The Life of St. Anthony*. (It was dedicated to the patron Saint of the Italians.)

More than 2500 people turned out as the curtain went up on a stage of old railroad ties and scrap lumber. Gentille played the role of the devil.

"Opera lovers from all over came, including the governor and mayor. And when the crowd had gone I went over to Mr. Terlizzo, the church custodian, and asked him what he thought.

"He said, 'Gendy, the Lord gave us a good day, but Mr. Yarusso, with God's help, gave us a good sunset.'"

"I never figured out until years later what he meant, but I think it was a fine piece of philosophy."

As we walked out onto the Avenue that day, Gendy said:

"People ask me many times why I write about the past. Perhaps it is a compulsion that makes me feel like I'm home again. When I walk down the old familiar streets, I begin to call out names of families who once lived in the old familiar places. But I would not want to come back and live there again.

"Memory is what enables man to survive and to progress. We don't like to see people we love taken away. For when they go, they take part of you with them."

But Gentille Yarusso left a lot of himself behind.

Of him it could be said: "With God's help, he gave us a sunset."

(March 31, 1980.)

Tiger Jack weathers times with secret success formula

On one of the hottest August afternoons I drove out to Dale Street and Interstate 94 to find out how my long-time friend, Tiger Jack Rosenbloom, "the World's Biggest Small Businessman," has been faring during the economic troubles.

"I been doin' just fine, Mr. Oliver," said Tiger Jack, who has raised, supported and helped eight children get ahead in the world from his 8-by-10 corrugated metal and wood hut, reputed to be the nation's smallest general store. From it, Tiger Jack sells hickory chips, charcoal, wood, Christmas trees in season, cosmetics, candies, small American flags, eggs, pop and sundries.

And, indeed, business was brisk on this stifling day in the hut, where two's a crowd. Tiger Jack stood in the back making change for a woman buying pop and candy. One more customer waited outdoors. A big fan humming from on top of the wood-and-coal stove kept everybody from being suffocated.

There is barely room for the small refrigerator filled with cans of pop and eggs. The "shelves" are boxes of candies and gum on packing cases. The sacks of coal and chips are stacked outside the door.

"Come on up to the corner," said Tiger. "I'm goin' to show you how things have been goin'. I own this corner and also where my shack and the car washing annex are located. I used to bring in a lot of produce every summer and stand out there and sell it or get my kids to sell it. Now, I just lease out the space to that fellow with the truck and he sells the produce. He makes a few dollars and I make some. Before I was doin' all the work. Now, we're both makin' something. That's the free enterprise system, Mr. Oliver."

He's washed a lot of cars and shined a lot of shoes on that corner and fought off winter's cold and snow and summer's heat and rain. But he looks the same at 68 as he did when I met him 20 years ago.

Tiger Jack, who claims to be a descendant of the Lost Tribes of Israel—"when Moses went east, my people went south"— has come a long way since he jumped out of a freight-train boxcar in 1936 after coming here from Columbus, Ohio.

"For eight days I lived at the old Union Gospel Mission and then I wandered into Colbert's gym in the Hamm Building and began to box and, Mr. Oliver, I have never been unemployed since. No sir. Please mention some of my great friends from those years: My Sullivan, he just died; Freddie Lenhart; Jimmy and Bob Watters; Smitty the policeman." His boxing days ended in 1946.

There was a shoeshine shack behind Cook's store at Sixth and Robert where Tiger Jack started out shining shoes and selling odds and ends.

"So I moved that building out here 33 years ago and I've been here ever since. Supported my family right outta here. All my kids are doing well and I've got 12 grandkids.

"Don't want to forget my wife, Mama Nurceal. She's been working at Miller and United Hospitals for 22 years."

Tiger Jack had to hustle. And as he hustled, he became one of the most respected people in the city's black community. His affable personality and ready philosophy bring customers from the most affluent districts in the most expensive cars to shop at Tiger's.

"Mr. Oliver, look at this letter. It says I got one of the highest credit ratings a businessman can get. People come here to see how I do it and they don't believe what they see. I've been on TV and the radio and in the papers all over the country."

"I'm trying to get my place here declared a national landmark."

"Folks always ask me, 'Tiger, what's the secret of your success?'

"It's no military secret. It's Tiger Jack's secret."
(August 24, 1982.)

A more likely traveling salesman story

It was the other noon at the Philosopher's Table in the Pioneer Coffee Shop and we had quorum of intellects befitting a Damon Runyon short story, as I recall. Jacob Dim, judge of bankruptcy court, was there and Harry Latz, Marvin Scherzer and Jules Braufman, all regulars.

But just lately we have added a new member, Abe Harris, who is stretching 80 and has been dubbed the story-teller and humorist because of his more than a half century as a traveling man, a drummer for the B. W. Harris clothing company. Abe leans more toward the ebullience of the

"Music Man's" Professor Harold Hill than Willy Loman in "Death of a Salesman." That is remarkable since Abe navigates in a walker because of some leg troubles.

Abe has been retired these last 11 years, but his memory is keen and when we have finished solving the world's problems, we turn to him for our dessert. Like that noon.

The hub of all of Abe's stories, of course, was the old B. W. Harris building at Sixth and Sibley (now Park Square Court) and from there he radiated with his pads of order blanks and trunks of samples, which caused many a small town drayman to groan when Abe got off some limited or local to "make the territory."

In the early 1920s, of course, Abe always went by train and his litany of the trains he traveled across the northern half of America is a recital of the best and worst, including cabooses, which he frequently tried.

"I sat in every parlor car, scrunched up in every berth, bounced in day coaches and ate in diners from here to there everywhere. Ah, who could forget the lunches and dinners in the elegance of diners on the North Coast Limited or Empire Builder, watching the passing landscape as the train plunged through a sunset, a blizzard, a rain storm, a moonlight night in the Rockies?"

Abe waxed lyrical at times about these things.

"The other side of the coin," says Abe. Threading your way through southeastern Minnesota—Lanesboro, Preston, Harmony, Decorah, Iowa, Austin, Spring Valley—it was a story of jerky locals and nights in small town hotels.

"We were kings, then. The arrival of the traveling salesman was the big event in a small town. He'd come twice a year, maybe. Everybody waited. We'd write letters to merchants in towns surrounding the county seat or the biggest town and then we'd set up our wares in the hotel sample rooms. The merchants would come in like it was carnival. 'Abe Harris is coming. Abe is coming,' they'd say up and down main street."

Some of those occasions were like carnivals. Ike Lederer, one of the most famous clothing salesmen in the business, says Abe, used to throw a big party for everybody in the town, almost.

"People appreciated the traveling salesman then. He brought business to town and the hotel loved it. They were always putting on big family-style meals in the dining room—platters of help-yourself pork chops, roast beef, baked ham, fried and baked chicken.

"You had to be imaginative and creative to get around in the years before every drummer switched to the automobile.

"I'd catch the morning or night passenger train to a town, set up my samples, make my sales. Instead of waiting around for the next through train to the next big city, I'd hop a local or freight to the town in between, call on my customers, catch a freight back and pick up the limited that night or next morning. That way I covered two towns in one day."

There was not always honor among salesmen competing for the small town buyer's buck.

"I never mentioned in the hotel that I was going to do this because salesmen had a way of leap-frogging ahead of you and they'd clean up the business before you arrived," says Abe.

"You had a choice on some lines of first, second or third-class tickets. I never found out what the difference was until one day we got into a sleet storm on a slight grade. The conductor came through the train and bawled 'All first-class passengers keep your seats. All second-class passengers get out and walk up the hill. Third-class get out and push.'"

Abe had finished his story of the day. As we prepared to adjourn, Harry Latz helped Abe into his walker and across the restaurant.

"I'm traveling second-class today," he called back.

"And I'm going third," said Harry, pushing.

(July 25, 1979.)

It's baked beans without franks

I climbed stairs I hadn't climbed in a dozen years. Near the top I was joined by ghosts. But the man waiting at the head of the stairs was real enough.

He was Ken Freiberg of Captain Ken's baked beans—and lately chili—wearing his genuine fireman's hat, which added to the grotesqueness of that winter's afternoon at 344 S. Robert St., the old Peters Meats empire.

Or doesn't anyone remember "Peters, the leaders," a slogan created by the late Q. J. (Quan) David, and sung on the air, read from huge billboards, touted by the late Cedric Adams over WCCO radio and TV?

Or the sausages and cold meats that peered up from every meat and fastfood counter?

The big billboard sign facing north toward the Loop, now tells of Captain Ken's Firehouse Baked Beans.

It is a strange melding of two dynasties—one having flourished and faded, the other still rising.

Both in my ken.

"That's a pun, son," said Ken, as we started exploring what were to me old paths and places in that once vast and yellow-stuccoed meat monarchy.

"Do you mind if the ghosts come, too?" I said.

"No, I feel them, too," he said.

We went up into the penthouse office, where Bill Peters, eldest of the brothers Bill, Ralph and Bob, had his office, with windows facing the Downtown skyline, and the Downtown St. Paul airport, and where Bill used to sit and watch the planes take off and land; below, on the tracks, the once classy Great Western railway passenger trains formerly ran.

We went into the big, mahogany paneled office, once the throne room of the Peters kingdom, now empty, chilly. But I could see Bob Peters sitting behind the desk, chain-smoking, taut as a spring, wearing his always-sporty checked suits, surrounded by his fabled art collection. Perhaps half million dollars worth of paintings once hung on the walls of the room, also filled with the aromas of smoking sausages and curing meats.

Over there hung Sir Joshua Reynolds' painting of Lady Olivia Carpenter. Nearby was a Nicolas Poussin and on the far wall an Andrea Del Sarto.

There were, in all, 130 pieces in the Peters collection.

I could hear Bob Peters' exultation about art, but it was Captain Ken speaking:

"Frankly, we're rattling around in this huge labyrinth of buildings and rooms, like the old Pierre Hotel over there, with its ornamental scrollwork. I'll bet you never knew it was there. Who has its history before Peters annexed it?"

Where the huge smokehouses stood—now long cool, faintly smelling of hickory wood smoke—two shifts of men and women cook, simmer, pack Firehouse baked beans and chili, little by little absorbing the space as success beckons. There is a reminiscent scent of smoking meats—the bacon, salt pork, the chili meat, steaming in cauldrons, where sausage was cooked.

"We were walking on top of each other up at 1814 Selby Ave. This place was available. I knew its history, the ghosts that haunt the place, even in broad daylight," says the former St. Paul fire captain, who created his products in Engine House 14, where I first ate them 15 years ago.

In the winter's afternoon sun, the flat-roofed collection of ivory buildings gleams like a modern Alhambra.

The ghosts won't be there when I go back.

(February 9, 1981.)

Super market—Corner store floats way to success

The two-story building with the split personality stands on the northeast corner of Fort Road and Randolph Avenue. The only curbside clues to its dual purpose are the date 1889 and the name Machovec at the peak of the slightly gingerbread, bay-window façade and the likeness of a river towboat, Sophie Rose, painted hugely across a brick wall on the corner, with a big, colorful buoy in a river of green, wavy lichen grass.

For 94 years, succeeding generations of Czech and German West Enders have used Machovec's as their personal neighborhood grocery and butcher shop. They have reveled in its cozy, Old World atmosphere, where poppy seeds are ground fresh each day, where you can speak Czech and be understood; they like the butcher who cuts meat to fit your needs and budget, admire the pressed ornamental ceiling supporting walls covered with gilt-framed family album portraits of all the Machovecs, starting with grandfather Frank C. Machovec.

They like to exchange the gossip of the day and banter with jolly Stanley Machovec, the third-generation owner, who sits at a rolltop desk in the clutter of a narrow office behind the meat department.

And they have no idea that this is the dividing line between friendly, old Machovec's and the other half of the operation: the largest, if not only, major Mississippi River supply center north of St. Louis.

Nor that jolly, affable Stan pushes out the back door tons and tons and pounds and pounds of meats, fresh green groceries, dry groceries, mountainous cases of mops, toilet paper, towels, soap powders, plastic wrap, garbage can liners, mops, buckets, pails, needles and thread, all of which supply hundreds of river tows and crews each year.

Unless you ask, he may forget to mention that he and his partner, Jim Dye, own three tows of their own—the Sophie Rose (named for Stan's mother), the Sadie Mae (named for Dye's mother-in-law) and the Dominique II, a huge diesel fuel and water supply barge.

Not to forget the four sleek vans used to haul supplies to dockside or ferry tow crews to and from locks downriver, to and from docks on the harbor front and to and from the airport.

"Any time day or night," says Stan.

Machovec's Boat Service and Store has come a long way since Stan put the first sacks of groceries and meats on a tow at Lambert landing in 1940, driving his father's delivery truck.

It is 3 p.m. on a Tuesday. The ship-to-shore radio is crackling in Stan's ear as he sits at his desk completing a huge order form for a tow that radioed in its needs earlier that day from near Winona.

The radio message is from another tow approaching Lake City. It will dock in St. Paul at midnight and the captain and one crewman need transport to the airport. Three others need lodging for the night.

"No sweat," says Stan into the microphone.

"One of our vans will take the two to the airport and the others can sleep in our guest house"—three bedrooms, lounge and complete bathroom-bathing facilities on the second floor of the west wing of the store, converted into comfortable hotel-like quarters.

The same tow's cook gets on the radio with a long order. She calls it in by numbers.

She has hardly done her "10-4" when Stan shoves the order form over to his son, Mike, 18, who takes it into the cavernous, stone-walled basement where all the dry groceries and canned goods are stored and where three huge freezers are brimming with choice cuts of meats.

"River tow crews eat nothing but the best and a lot of it," says Stan.

The radio crackles again. A tow near Hastings Lock No. 2 is tied up there for unloading and needs fuel oil quickly and also water.

That's where the Sophie Rose, Sadie Mae and Dominique II come in. One of them will nudge the loaded fuel barge downriver from the Koch Oil Tank Farm below Shepard Road.

In this case it's the Sadie Mae, and Stan and I get into one of his vans to drive to the landing to watch the drama.

On the way, Stan fills in more of the story.

"You see, not all the tows come this far upstream, so we go to them with our vans and tows," says Stan. "Like a few weeks ago, the river was closed up here for four days by high water. Then it's low water. We had 14 boats to service in one weekend." Machovec's Boat Service enjoys so much popularity on the river because it is unique and does every kind of service task.

"Night before last, we got a radio message that a tow had broken down near Lock No. 2 and needed parts. I got two vans out by 8 the next morning, sending each to parts suppliers we have listed. By 8:30 a.m., they'd returned to the store, and we sent one van with all the parts to the boat. We had it all delivered by 9 a.m."

Nor is any request beyond fulfilling. Stan's wife, Gloria, often leaves their Cottage Grove home and shops for clothes for the crews.

"A guy lost his luggage at the airport. We retrieved it and drove 100 miles—to below Winona—and delivered it to him."

"We sold a million gallons of diesel fuel in that thing last year," says Stan as we watch Sadie Mae's skipper Jack Meeks pull the fuel barge out into the channel and start it downriver.

"He'll be unloading that fuel in 30 minutes," said Stan.

We drove back to the store, stopping to inspect a warehouse filled with more supplies, coils of rope, parts, pumps, and winches.

Back in the store, the front half, Stan's oldest daughter, Linda, was checking out meat and groceries for a man in his 80s who spoke with a rich Czech accent. He said he just couldn't understand how Machovec's could compete with the big supermarkets. But thank goodness, it was still there.

"You just don't know the half of it," said Stan.
(June 15, 1983.)

Northfield Touring history

Twenty years ago, if someone had suggested a day-long walking tour of downtown Northfield and environs without leaving the Victorian age of architecture, the reaction from the City Fathers might have been: "Let's modernize!"

Fortunately, only a token of such work was done. This venerable old town with two formidable colleges—Carleton and St. Olaf—boasts of 65 buildings built between 1858 and 1909.

And Northfield residents have been quick to take advantage of this tourist attraction in the current wave of nostalgic preservation rolling across the land.

A generous slice of Old Northfield has been designated the Northfield Historic District by the U. S. Interior Department. And come the second weekend in May, during National Preservation and Restoration Month, Northfield will cut a ribbon on a "walk through history" that will blend not only historic façades but a vast collection of boutiques, art and antique shops, jewelry and craft stores and a fine and performing arts center.

The tour begins in the Northfield Historical Society offices in the 1868-era Scriver building on Bridge Square, This is also the old First National Bank, where the James Younger gang made infamous history in 1876. Here is the exact replica of that bank on that day. And also here is Mrs. Virginia (Ginny) Mondale, Northfield Historical Society director, from whose desk the tours start and where you get all the brochures, T-shirts and souvenirs.

Here are some of the tour stops, most of them along the main thoroughfare—Division Street:

• No. 315-17 Division Street is the French building (1873), housing two picturesque Northfield institutions— the Ideal Cafe, where Northfield "coffees" twice a day, and Willie's Shoe Repair, where the patriarchs of Northfield gather to chat and doze amid a conglomeration of leather repair machinery and leather goods in various stages of repair.

• The Carnegie Library, 3rd and Division, circa 1910, is typical of such architecture. Librarian Marston Headley, pleasant and chatty town historian, is usually found in the Pye Room of historical material.

• The Stuart Hotel at 212 Division originally was opened in 1877 as the Archer House by the Kahler (hotel) family. It has been given a huge boost by the announcement that Colonial Properties, its present owners, have agreed to restore, refurbish and preserve the French Second Empire chateau-styled landmark.

The managing and renewal will be done by Jeanne Hall of the Anderson Hotel family in Wabasha. And she plans a riverfront dining room, pub, 27 or 28 rooms and complete Victorian graciousness in decor and living. Famed Anderson Hotel-family cooking will be a bonus.

• The 1873-Nutting Block at 220 Division retains its Ro-manesque exterior and inside is the Dittmann Travel Agency.

• The original city hall next door (302 Division) was erect-ed in 1880 and, appropriately, is an antiques shop now.

• The gem may be the old YMCA building at 304 Division, which went up in 1885 and a year ago was acquired by the Northfield Arts Guild. The Guild turned its three floors (featuring a two-story bay window) into an art gallery which displays the works of local artists and craftsmen.

Back on Bridge Square, the obvious commercial "palaces" stare you in the face:

On the Central Block, southeast corner, is Northfield's "leviathan" and largest commercial building in town. It's three stories and is Queen Anne style with Romanesque mode and corner turret. Admire the terra cotta designs on the columns, capitals and bases. Contrastingly, the corner ground floor is occupied by an avant-garde record shop run by some young ex-St. Olaf students.

Kitty-corner in the Nutting/Phillips building (1889) is the present First National Bank. (It has been there since 1893.)

About now it is time to search out a place for lunch. Since the prestigious Les Quatre Amis closed a few months ago, the luxury choices are limited. But there are Marty's in the new Riverfront Mall and the Rueb-n'-Stein at 503 Division (both with a sort of collegiate atmosphere and fares featuring salads, sandwiches, burgers, big steaks and chops). Next door to the Rueb-n'-Stein is Lano's Takara Jima Oriental restaurant, better than most.

Having lunched, a little exploring off Division nets further glimpses into Northfield's amazingly well preserved past:

Just east up Fourth, off Bridge Square, past the former Quatres Amis, is the granddaddy of them all: the yellow clapboard with a V-roof Lyceum building. It's the town's oldest and was built in 1857 by John North, Northfield's founder. You probably won't get a tour now unless you have a toothache because it presently houses a dental office.

At the corner of Fourth and Washington is the Grand Theater (Ware Auditorium), of 1899 vintage. It's a structure designed in the Federal Revival era by widely known

Minneapolis architect Harry Carter, who created Palladian windows, pilasters, balconies and floor plan of a proscenium theater of great status.

Back down Fifth to Division and heading toward Bridge Square, these classics:

• The Scofield building (1870), southeast corner, is one of the best-preserved cast iron-façade structures in the state and similar to those in the Soho district of New York City. The nameplate at the top is simple: "The Store."

• One more historic monument lies across the Cannon River, west of Bridge Square: The Malt-O-Meal plant, site of John North's grist and sawmill built in 1855-56. The 1873 portion survives as part of the Malt-O-Meal factory, which still turns out the internationally eaten "Northfield porridge."

(April 4, 1980.)

Bishop Whipple keeps sturdy handhold

Betty Oehler almost forgot about the portrait of Queen Victoria, the one hanging on the staircase at 921 Goodrich Ave. and autographed to her great grandfather.

"Presented to Bishop Henry Whipple at Windsor Castle, Nov. 10th, 1890, by Victoria Regina," the inscription says.

And that reminded Betty to get out the big picture/story book of Queen Victoria's family and life at Balmoral Castle in the Scottish Highlands, the cover properly embossed with the royal seal and crest and the frontispiece again addressed to Bishop Whipple from Her Majesty in 1892.

Both the bishop and the queen ended their stewardships in the same year—1901.

"Victoria loved to hear about the 'Indians,'" Betty says, apologizing for having almost forgotten about two of the most valuable memorabilia collected by her illustrious great grandfather. Part of that vast collection of Sioux and Chippewa artifacts has now been brought together in a premier exhibit at the Science Museum of Minnesota.

That is why I recently went to chat with Betty, wife of prominent attorney Cole Oehler. She had a great deal to do with the Bishop Whipple exhibit.

"When you have lived all your life with a man like Henry Whipple always in your background and your family's background, you begin to take for granted these vastly valuable things like Victoria's portrait or the picture book," Betty said.

The progeny that Mrs. Oehler's grandmother, Jane Whipple, the bishop's daughter, spawned when she married Henry Alexander Scandrett were rather imposing, too.

Betty's father, Benjamin, was executive vice president of the Northern Pacific railway and his brother, her Uncle Henry "ran the Milwaukee railroad as president for years."

"Well, believe me, Bishop Whipple—we always called him 'the Bish'—cropped-up everywhere in our daily lives and he always has and he always will," she says.

"Even though I never knew him. But he comes back to us in strange ways like our granddaughter, Alicia, being baptized in St. Cornelia's Episcopal church at St. Charles, Minn., which her great-great-great-grandfather consecrated and named after his first wife, Cornelia."

The bishop was, she believes, one of the nation's greatest missionaries of good works, humanitarianism and Christianity.

"And that's what makes him so fascinating. There is no place in this whole world where he didn't travel, spreading the 'good news' and doing what he could to make people comfortable and happier."

He baptized a Harvard graduate in the River Jordan, missionized in Africa and dropped the "seed of Episcopalianism" like a Christian Johnny Appleseed.

He consecrated churches in St. Paul including St. John's and Christ Episcopal. He was a founder of St. Luke's hospital (now part of United Hospitals). He established the historic wood frame Episcopal church in Northfield and another mission church among the Sioux at Prairie Island near Red Wing.

He supported Episcopalian schools too — Breck in the Twin Cities, Shattuck, St. James, St. Mary's and Seabury Divinity schools in Faribault.

And when he settled down in Faribault he founded the Cathedral there as the "headquarters church" across the street from the old Whipple home, which has been torn down.

"So actually, St. Mark's in Minneapolis was founded to accommodate the huge Twin Cities' area populations, but in his eyes and mind, *the* Cathedral at Faribault was always the Cathedral," Betty says.

And it is in the Faribault Episcopal Cathedral that Bishop Whipple is buried, near his chapel, "where all of us children always went to pray whenever we visited the family home."

But most of all the Bishop is remembered for his love and respect for the Indians.

"You know, he loved to talk about his friends, the Indians, even more than (about) Queen Victoria."
(December 3, 1980.)

Century-old chief scowls again in Stillwater

A popular and respected Stillwater resident who disappeared more than 40 years ago is back in town as a summer visitor. The mysterious tale of his career, disappearance and discovery-recovery by two super sleuths is now a part of the romantic legends of the river city.

The story begins in 1882, when Byron J. Mosier opened a cigar store on the northeast corner of Main and Chestnut streets in downtown Stillwater.

Like barbershops and their barber poles, no cigar store with status could be without its cigar store Indian.

Mosier had his sculpted out of fine woods, finished with exquisite varnishes and polishes and installed just to the right of the front door.

There Chief Stillwater stood to be admired as a landmark for 60 years.

He was a majestic person—nearly 8 feet tall.

Mosier got him from Chicago.

Grown men recall sitting on his knee as children, posing on the base with wheels, on which he stood. Old family albums are filled with photos of people with Chief Stillwater.

It was the thing to do to have your picture taken with him. That stern, stoic countenance never wavered.

He became a landmark, beloved and cherished by an entire town.

No vandal ever even scratched a wooden match on his costume.

Then one day in the 1940s, the chief was missing—only to turn up again at the Lowell Inn.

Then, not long afterwards, he was gone from there, too, as if he had been whisked into the mists of the St. Croix.

The return of the native is mostly the effort of Stillwater historian and writer Anita Buck.

It was Anita who played the role of Miss Marple, with assistance from another ace detective, Louise Johnson, retired curator of the Washington County Historical Society.

Louise shared Anita's curiosity and inquisitiveness about the chief. "I'm not sure how he left the Lowell Inn," says Anita. "But it wasn't easy. He weighs 300 pounds."

He may have been kidnapped or merely purloined, or even just loaned out by Nelle Palmer, who owned the inn then.

"In any event, we lost track of him for some years. But I was just determined enough to want him back to pursue my detective work," says Anita.

Cigar store Indians were becoming collector's items, valuable and sought-after antiques.

Besides, not every town could boast of having one as a resident.

When she and Johnson finally picked up some clues, it took a strange and fascinating path from the Lowell Inn to Southdale Shopping Center, the Dayton (department store) family and, eventually, the Minnesota State Historical Society. It was a picture magazine article in 1956 at the grand opening of Southdale that provided the first evidence.

"In one of the photos, some people were standing alongside a cigar store Indian alongside a kiosk," says Anita.

But she didn't see it until much later, when someone who knew of her quest sent a copy.

As Anita pieced together the story from there, it went something like this:

George Nelson Dayton got the chief as a birthday present sometime in the late 1940s. That's how it turned up in Southdale, where Dayton's located a major store; that's also how it must have been seen in front of B. Dalton, part of the Dayton Hudson Corp.

Dayton died in 1950 and, in a letter written to Anita Buck, his son Donald said that when his father's estate was being settled, the chief was among the assets.

Dayton wrote that he and his four brothers drew lots for the chief, and Donald won.

He moved it to Southdale then, where it stood until he heard Washington County was trying to get the chief back. He says, in his letter, that he offered it to Washington County, but whomever he reached did not seem interested.

Anita says she couldn't imagine who that might have been.

So instead Dayton donated it to the Minnesota Historical Society, which accepted Chief Stillwater as a gift.

There he has remained in his crate.

Apprised of this development, Anita and Louise and a plethora of interested Washington County historical buffs appealed to the historical society for the chief's return.

The society explained it could not do so without legislative, legal hocus-pocus. But what it could do was loan the chief to Washington County for a time, if the county would provide its distinguished guest comfortable quarters and maintenance.

This was done with financial direction by Charlotte Robledo, treasurer of the Washington County Historical Society, and grants from the First National Bank of Stillwater, Washington Federal Savings and Loan, the Cosmopolitan State Bank, Norwest Bank of Stillwater and the Margaret Rivers Fund.

Thus, not long ago, came "travel orders" for Chief Stillwater from Marcia Anderson, curator of collections at the State Historical Society.

Chief Stillwater will be a resident until Oct. 31 in the appropriate salon of the Washington County Historical Society museum, presided over by curator Yvette Bergeron Handy.

She says the "return of the native"—in mint condition, standing stalwart, tomahawk raised in a gesture of peaceful courage—already has become a tourist attraction.

Detectives Buck and Johnson have not yet been offered jobs by the FBI.

(May 26, 1986.)

Cooks mix up a memorial

They call themselves La Societe de Cuisine des Amis de V.E.M.—the cooking society of the friends of Verna E. Meyer.

But there are less formal titles, such as "Verna's Girls" and, more humorously, "Verna's Leftovers."

It is as strange a memorial to a friend and teacher as it is convivial and tasty.

Once a month, 10 to 15 members living in the Twin Cities area gather in each other's kitchens on a rotating basis to cook in the memory of Mrs. Meyer, who died two years ago and was their friend and culinary mentor—for some for more than a quarter century.

She always called them "Verna's Girls."

They had taken every course she offered, from beginning cooking through the most complicated recipes mindful of Escoffier at his finest. She took them around the world in their kitchens.

For many years, she taught classes in the Minneapolis YWCA, but her most popular location was in Lutece cookware store in St. Louis Park. In the 1970s, Verna taught as many as six classes a week, at all levels and for men as well as women.

Verna retired in 1977 and suggested, for auld lang syne, that this hard core of "girls" continue in a sort of private, exclusive group, meeting in their kitchens to chat, cook, eat and enjoy their company.

Verna, of course, was the catalyst, the creator of each menu.

They come from diverse and widely scattered backgrounds—wives of doctors, high-tech executives, wives of lawyers, a culinary shop manager, teachers, single business women, librarians. One, Mae Horns, is a famous marathon runner.

One of them is my wife.

Some were members of the Twin Cities Wine and Food Society, of which Verna was a charter member and leader. Others had gone with her on frequent food forays through Europe.

It was a love of good food and good cooking plus the love of their teacher that brought them together in the first place.

When Verna died at 86, the "Girls" discussed suitable monuments and memorials.

Let's continue as we have, in her memory, they decided.

Much of what they cook are Verna's leftovers. (In fact, the group is putting together a cookbook of Verna's leftover recipes and menus, plus some members' recipes.)

Whatever it is, the hostess of the day makes the menu and recipe decisions. She buys all the raw materials. When the "Leftovers" arrive on the second Wednesday of each month, usually starting about 10 a.m., the hostess has copies of the day's recipes and menu, plus assignments for each member. For two hours they slice, peel, bake, poach, broil, mix, and create sauces, dressings.

They take off their aprons, the hostess opens the wine and offers the first toast to Verna Meyer.

Verna's presence is never far away. The first time they met after her death, it was at the home of Kathy Gretsch in North Oaks. She had planned the menu some time before Verna's passing. They had expected her to be there. Instead, it became their "memorial service" to her. It was at that meeting they decided to carry on.

When they got to the dessert, Grand Marnier soufflé with sauce Parisienne and strawberries, somebody happened to read what Verna had written at the bottom of the recipe:

"If someone invited me to their house and served me a Grand Marnier soufflé for dessert, I'd know they really loved me."

(February 25, 1985.)

Norske-Torske Club (almost) strictly Norwegian

Shattering old stereotypes is hard work.

Like the one about St. Paul being an Irish town.

You'd never believe that one if you dropped into a St. Paul Norske-Torske Klubben (Norske-Torske Club) lunch in the Prom Center one Saturday almost every month. You'd think it was a Viking invasion.

I saw it all with my own eyes.

This is no gathering of Norwegians trying for a foothold in the land of leprechauns. This is a full-scale revolution and takeover.

What brings them together is fish—cod called Torsk in their native tongue.

The notion that all the Norskies in Minnesota fill that section west of the Lefse Curtain in Minneapolis is another folk tale without substance.

The St. Paul Norske-Torske Klubben is the largest in the United States. Three hundred members turn out nine times a year (torsk doesn't keep well in summer).

Another 100 men are waiting in the wings to fill any empty chairs.

If you miss twice without a good excuse, out you go.

"The Sons of Norway in Minneapolis is like a Ladies Aid Society compared to the St. Paul Norske-Torske," Merlin Kvaal, the program chairman, told me.

I had been invited to talk on "The Care and Cleaning of Torsk and Lutefisk, Fish of Kings." (Lutefisk is dried cod, cured with lye. Like parachuting, you should try it once. They don't eat it at the Norske-Torske club. They just talk about it.)

I hadn't seen so many Norwegians since I was in Oslo several years ago. There were even more Norwegians in that huge Prom Center than there are at St. Olaf College.

"When we formed 14 years ago, we had to go through the phone book to find Norwegians," Kvaal said. "Nobody in St. Paul wanted to admit they were Norwegian."

My appearance as an on-again, off-again ethnic German created some talk of heresy.

"Name some Norwegians," someone said at the door, "or we'll banish you to O'Gara's pub."

So I named some Norwegians—Ole Bull, Ole Rolvaag, Edvard Munch, King Olav and Dave Johnson, who always gets me the tickets to St. Olaf College's Christmas festival.

"He's no Norwegian," said Merlin of Johnson. "After 40 years as college vice president, he's been unmasked as a Swede."

They should have known because Johnson always spelled it ludefisk instead of lutefisk and wanted cream sauce instead of melted butter on his fish.

Once limited to pureblooded Norwegians, there are even some Swedes and Danes in the membership. Bank executives of Swedish origin, such as Glen Olson of American National, have been palming themselves off as Norwegians for years. Olson had worked his way up to the head table.

At another table was Len Halper, the only Jewish-Norwegian, who had brought as his guest and potential member, insurance executive "Irish" Charley O'Leary.

"Instead of a purely ethnic club, we have become a prestigious club of leading business and professional people, all at the top," Kvaal said.

"For instance, if the roof fell in this noon and all were lost, everybody on the corporate ladder in the Twin Cities would move up a notch."

But the conviviality of the occasion centers on torsk, and to a lesser degree the aquavit and Norwegian beer. Batting practice at the bar lasts about an hour and then, at a command from Kaare Rosenberg, everybody shouts:

"Bring on the torsk!" (which is really Boston scrod).

A regiment of waitresses appears, laden with platters of steamy fish, then boiled potatoes, pitchers of hot melted butter, Norwegian rye, lefse, aquavit and beer for constant toasting.

There are seconds and sometimes thirds.

They sing Norwegian Viking songs. They have Norwegian programs, given by Germans and Poles.

When they sing the Norwegian national anthem, tears roll down their cheeks.

And you call this an Irish town?

(April 15, 1983.)

History, memories fill up old buildings at St. Kate's

Two of my favorite buildings on the College of St. Catherine campus, Derham Hall and Our Lady of Victory Chapel, have just achieved status on the National Register of Historic Places. But for hundreds of "Katies" and Derham "dollies," this recognition is only what they've all known for more personal and sentimental reasons.

And this had nothing to do with the age or architectural qualities of either building, but rather the day-by-day drama of how their lives were changed in the corridors, rooms and awesome quiet of the chapel.

They probably could not recite the details of the Romanesque collegiate, turn-of-the-century design of Derham Hall, nor the fact it was built in 1904 and '05 as the very first building on campus, housing the young ladies who became the first students at the College of St. Catherine. They may not know that somehow, without the walls bulging, it also managed to provide space for Derham Hall High School, not to mention the nuns, the chapel, dining rooms and unforgettable bathtubs in the clammy, cold basement.

Only vaguely does any of them remember that the hall is named for a prosperous Irish Catholic farmer named Hugh

Derham, from Rosemount (he named the town, too), who contributed the $20,000 needed to erect the four-story structure, or that the architect was John Wheeler, a relative of Archbishop John Ireland, who designed numerous other buildings in Minnesota for the Sisters of St. Joseph.

Nor would a lot of the past and present generations on campus identify the chapel with 1924, when it was consecrated and dedicated. They would only know that, by coincidence, both National Register buildings are linked by an enclosed cloister arch that resembles the famed Rialto Bridge across the Grand Canal of Venice and that the modern Katie refers to as "the original St. Paul skyway."

Oh, and a lot of them will know that the chapel of Byzantine Romanesque beauty is where they were married, where their daughters and granddaughters have been married and where they went to pray for good grades, worthy husbands and successful careers.

When I mentioned the news about the buildings to my wife, a Derham "dolly" of a few years ago, her memories were not about the regal elegance of the entrance foyer between the lofty Grecian columns, the softly lighted parlors with their ornamental ceilings and stained glass. Instead, she recalled wryly how she had sat in Sister Mary William's English class, at a desk near the rear of the room with a good window view of the Dew Drop lake, and daydreamed of things far afield from the conjugation of verbs. For us, the chapel has special meaning because of its likeness to the Cathedral of St. Trophime (also spelled Tromphime) in Arles, France, which is the inspiration for Our Lady of Victory.

Sister Mary William, by the way, is now the archivist for the college, and the other afternoon she gathered together not only files, but two early Derham Hall "dollies," for my inquiries.

Sister Immaculata Keenan was a high school freshman in 1924 and Sister Marie Inez Johnson a senior that same year. "I had entered as a non-Catholic, and my mother, in fact, was somewhat dubious about what would happen to me. But she went to see what it was all about and came back to say, 'Girls, it's not going to be too bad; I hear the nuns laughing,'" said Sister Marie Inez.

To go farther back: "You have to understand," Sister Mary William said, "that Derham Hall was built for the college. But we had to have a feeder cadre, so we brought over some high school seniors from St. Joseph's Academy that January of 1905. They formed the nucleus of the college. We graduated our first two college seniors in 1911. And until 1915, when Whitby (College Hall) was built, this was both high school and college."

And never the twain shall meet, recalled sisters Marie Inez and Immaculata, whose recollections of Derham Hall and the chapel have little to do with the architecture or interior design of either.

"It was forbidden for high schoolers to associate with the college girls under penalty of being 'campused,' or worse," said Marie Inez.

Immaculata was a "townie"—she lived at home. Inez was a boarder.

Sister Mary Aloysius, principal for some years, used to tell how the "townies" would run down to the Dew Drop lake at noon and push each other in. Then they'd run back and say they had to go home and get clean clothes.

"I caught on to that one," she once said. "I made them wrap in blankets, come back up and wash, dry and iron their uniforms before they could go home."

That laundry room on the ground floor was a nightmare. It also housed the bathtubs and lavatories, and the girls would take turns coming down for their "Saturday night baths." Sister Flavia was the "chaperone and attendant." She sat on a bench, saying the Rosary, interjected by shouts: "Hail Mary, full of grace—Louise, you get out of that tub at once; Joyce, your turn, and hurry and wash your ears. Blessed art thou amongst women and—Virginia, you girls quit giggling and dry off and let somebody else use those tubs."

The chapel is Sister Antonia's real monument to the future of the college, they agreed.

"It is said that the chapel is built on one of the highest points of ground in the Twin Cities," said Sister Mary William. "And Sister Antonia wanted it to be constructed as much of materials found in Minnesota as possible. The façade is of Bedford travertine stone; there is Mantorville travertine on the interior and also Nemadji tile."

She hired H.A. Sullwold as the architect, but then toured Europe to view cathedrals and churches for design inspiration.

"When she got to Arles and saw St. Trophime, she had found the inspiration she needed," Sister Mary William said.

(February 12, 1986.)

Villa to note heritage

As Sister Borgia Fehig put it, "They've never seen anything like it before in the Cathedral of St. Paul and they probably will never see anything like it again." Sister Borgia, who is the superior of the Ursuline Sisters at Villa Maria in Old Frontenac, Minn., was referring to a 450th birthday celebration of the order's founding next Sunday afternoon in the Cathedral that will bring together a potpourri of people that would astound even the most ecumenical of ecumenists.

Certainly nothing like it has ever been scheduled before in that citadel of Catholicism.

She ticked off who will be there: Lutherans, Buddhists, Muslims, Ashrams, Presbyterians, Methodists, Congregationalists, Jews, and Mohammedans.

"And even a few Catholics," she chuckled.

"Like hundreds of our alumnae when the Villa was a prestigious boarding school for young women," said Sister M. Catherine McCarrick.

"Archbishop John Roach will concelebrate our birthday Mass," said Sister Albeus Coffey. "His sister was a student at the Villa."

The three nuns, among the 14 at the Villa, explained the reason for such a display of ecumenism.

These invited guests are a cross-section of the thousands of people of all races, creeds, backgrounds who have come to the Villa Maria Retreat Center since it rose from the ashes of a disastrous fire in 1969 that destroyed the school building and closed the school. But it left untouched the magnificent, three-story French provincial main building that is cloistered in the quiet woods of Old Frontenac on the Mississippi; just off U.S. Highway 61 near Lake City. Not to mention almost 200 richly appointed sleeping rooms with unrivaled views.

What might have been a prophecy of disaster "became, like Moses and the burning bush, a message from God to change," as Sister Catherine puts it.

Fortunately, the Ursulines got the message.

Hardly had the last graduating class made a tearful exit after almost a century of educating young women than a Lutheran minister named the Rev. Ham Muus showed up one day. He suggested to the nuns that the Villa would be an ideal locale for groups to get away from the noise of the world for brief periods. He offered to schedule the first such retreat.

He also made a rather unorthodox appearance, having arrived late at night and sleeping in his car so as not to disturb the sisters. However, sighting what appeared to be an unoccupied car in their parking lot, the sheriff was summoned and was about to haul Muus off to jail when Sister Emmanuel ran out.

"Do you claim this man?" said the sheriff.

"I certainly do," said Sister Emmanuel, thus adding to the lore and legend of the Villa.

Muus' idea, oddly enough, dovetailed exactly with the message of Sister Angela Merici, who founded the Ursuline order in 1535 in Brescia, Italy, and who will be honored at Sunday's ceremonies.

"Before we leaped, we looked up what Sister Angela had written and found these words," said Sister Catherine.

"If with change of times and circumstances, it becomes necessary to make fresh rules or to alter anything, then do it with prudence after taking good advice."

"That's all the Imprimatur we needed," said Sister Albeus, who is otherwise known as the "booking agent."

Under her quiet promotion, the center has become one of the largest of its kind in the United States and its bookings fill every weekend except Christmas and Easter.

"The only advertising has been done by God," she says.

The complexion of the groups ranges from Ashrams and Muslims to Catholics, social workers from around the world and "next year we're even going to have the TOPS—Take off Pounds Sensibly," Sister Albeus says.

Here, where the first Mass was celebrated at Fort Beauharnois in what is now Minnesota, social service workers from throughout the world were mingling with those at a Lutheran seminar.

All with Villa connections have been invited to be in the Cathedral for the 4 p.m. Mass of reunion. The alumnae also are in charge of the reception that follows in the Hall of Angels.

"We have also been visited by and heard from the descendants of our first graduate, Margaret Rahilly, class of 1892. And they have given us her graduation medal, which is here in the museum case," says Sister Catherine.

Sunday's ecumenism theme will be set by the Calvary Lutheran Church adult choir, which will perform a short concert before the Mass and lead the procession of entrance, which will include some 18 to 20 Ursulines as the guests of honor. St. John Vianney seminarians will assist with the music during the Mass, and "there will be congregational singing throughout," says Sister Albeus.

Roger Burg, Cathedral organist, will preside over the mighty Skinner pipe organ.

"We want this to be a real religious bash—an experience," says Sister Borgia.

"And," adds Sister Catherine, "we want the outside world beyond the Villa Maria to know that adversity can be overcome and that He who gives us the crosses also brings the blessings."

(October 16, 1985.)

Old West Side Flats gone but not forgotten

They sat in the sunshine of the 23rd floor at fashionable 740 River Drive and talked about a neighborhood and a time they no longer could see, except in their minds' eyes. Each man in the room had reached myriad success in fame, wealth or civic leadership and community service. Yet words like "poor" and "frugal" and "struggling to exist" kept coming into their conversation.

The place they scanned in memory was called in Yiddish a "Shtetl," a little village. But the city knew it as the Old West Side Flats. You won't find it on the map anymore. The Riverview Industrial Park erased all the traces and gave it a modern name.

But the men in the room that Sunday—in their 70s and 80s, have everything etched indelibly.

Their conversational images roamed along streets named Kentucky, Robertson, Fairfield, Eva and State, and across those collections of little, wood frame, paint-shy houses with narrow, fenced-in lots, where they all lived. They savored names like Goldberg's Market, Mintz's Shoe Store, Kessel's Bakery and Sunday mornings that were busier than Saturday nights on most main streets.

They had come, these men and their ancestors, for many reasons and from many countries, many persecutions, and many Russian pogroms, to find the promise still held out in the arms of the Statue of Liberty.

"They came," as Hy Edelman, the attorney said, "in search of freedom to live as they chose and when they got here, they were torn with the frustrations of trying to maintain a Jewish life in the Shtetl and still take advantage of the fruits of that freedom beyond Robert Street.

"The rabbis exhorted them not to desert their Jewishness and the children went to the university and studied in the libraries and discovered they could do something besides being peddlars, storekeepers, rabbis or teachers in the temple."

Now, in the sunny room at the pinnacle of fashionable living in the city, the patriarchs looked down that long road, sustained by ample portions of bagels and lox, served by their hostess, Ruth Lipschultz, whose husband, the late Sam Lipschultz, was one of the heroes who came off the Flats as a lawyer and civic and business leader.

Ralph Stacker has the floor and microphone of the tape recorder held by Dr. Bill Bernstein, himself a distinguished surgeon, "but of the old 13th Street neighborhood, the elite ghetto." Ralph Stacker's father ran the famous Lebanon Kosher Supply Co. food store at 248 E. Fairfield Ave. That was long before Ralph became a widely-respected St. Paul attorney.

"I worked for my dad. So did Hy Applebaum—you, Hy, over there (indicating Hy Applebaum of the Applebaum supermarket chain)—worked for nothing in my dad's grocery. I worked the herring barrel. Every Jewish mama thought the best herring were at the bottom of the barrel. I had to reach my arm way down through the brine and herring to get out the ones at the bottom. . . and then I'd run to catch the Robert Street streetcar for the university and law school. I smelled up the streetcar with those herring hands. Finally, it got so bad in class I took a change of clothes. I was shunned."

Roy Corwin's father was Cohen—Max Cohen, the Boss Tweed of the West Side Flats Tammany Hall. Roy changed his name to Corwin.

"We had lots of name changes. Anyway, my father was the political king of the Flats, of the Shtetl. Boss O'Connor ran the city. All Democrats. The breweries were big factors in politics. So a few weeks before an election, our basement mysteriously would be filled with beer," says Roy, "to per-suade the voters.

"On election day, the voting booth for the Third Precinct, Sixth Ward, was next to Ralph Stacker's dad's store. My dad would take the new immigrants into the booth and show them how to write in the names. They couldn't read or write. If there were 311 voters, the Democrats always got 310 and the Republicans one to make it look good."

Roy, who became a manufacturer and industrialist in the city (Roy Craft), remembered how he began, as a boy, working for G. Sommers Wholesaler, who had a warehouse on the West Side, where they stored all the Fourth of July fireworks.

"You could buy all you wanted almost for free on the 3rd of July if you worked there," he said.

"So one year, I took a bunch home and a pinwheel got lit. The sparks set off all the fireworks on our porch. There were rockets zooming off the porch all over the neighbor-hood. The mamas were screaming; the kids were cheering and the Fire Department was mad because we called the firemen out on a holiday to put out the fire on our porch."

Oscar Melamed, at 85, the senior among the patriarchs that morning and founder of Coast-to-Coast Stores, took the microphone:

"Our families came from Russia and Poland, Romania, the Ukraine and Germany in the 1880s. We got started, our fathers, by renting a horse and wagon from a man named Smith. And if we couldn't afford that, we rented a pushcart.

"From such a little thing, from a little store on Roberts Street came Coast-to-Coast. But are we happier today in all our luxury, now that we've got it made? I don't think so. I think we were happier then. Those were fabulous times. We were poor but never in poverty.

"Never did anyone go hungry or in need on the Flats. You all remember. Some of your folks were people about whom I am talking. We had our own welfare program. There was a Jewish refugee house. People in need, with sudden losses, penniless immigrants, they came to the Refugee House. Everybody contributed anonymously. The rabbi kept the books. You could pay it back, but you never paid interest and you never knew who had donated."

There was Ben Binstock, who at 84 has become an expert wood carver since he retired from the men's clothing business. He recalled how he used to fill his pockets with nails and pound them into the wooden sidewalks in front of his house so the walk would look shiny.

Then there was the artesian well at the end of Kentucky Street, where "we all got our drinking water and the horses drank from the trough next to it—and on dark nights, we'd get the two mixed up. When the floods came in Spring, we boys nailed together rafts from debris and ferried furniture and belongings for people whose houses were under water."

"I have to tell you how the West Side Flats really got its name," said Alex Tankenoff, a real estate developer in St. Paul (Metro Square, Hillcrest Shopping Center among others).

"We lived in a shabby fourplex on St. Lawrence Street and anything east of the railroad track toward what is now the airport was called the East Side Flats and everything west of the tracks was the West Side Flats. Most of the houses were west. That's my version."

Somebody mentioned "Der Verschwundener Maenner." Every Sabbath eve the old ladies would go to Stacker's store and buy copies of Yiddish newspapers from Chicago and New York and look for the page where there were photos and stories about men who had left families in Europe and come to this country, promising to send for their wives and children. Only some never did—the "Verschwundener Maenner" (Lost Men).

"The mamas would stand on the steps of the synagogues every Saturday and compare faces with photos in the papers and if they spotted one, they'd hang on to him until they could notify his family back in the Old Country," said Stacker.

Such went the banter that day at the top of 740 River Drive. They spoke of legends who swirled out of the Flats to fame and fortune such as Marty Capp of Capp homes, Arthur O. Dietz of CIT Financial Co., who persuaded Henry Ford he could sell cars on credit. There were the Lipschultz brothers, the Applebaums, and Alfred Perlman, who became president of the New York Central Railway in its palmy days.

The men in the room strained their eyes eastward across the cityscape, looking in vain for that which they knew no longer exists. Urban renewal and progress wiped it all away and life in the Shtetl had vanished by 1970—except for those memories like those shared that Sunday about when there was still laughter, tears, the cacophony of families on holidays, warm kitchens filled with love and (doughy) knishes.

(December 10, 1979.)

More Minnesota Memories

Whether you call it Greater or Out-state Minnesota, the towns near and beyond the seven county metropolitan area are filled with interesting people and places. Here are some of them.

Couple's efforts far-reaching

Lindstrom. They live these days in a comfortable little rambler on the north end of Elm Street, far away from the sight and sound of the traffic coursing through downtown Lindstrom, Minn., on U.S. Highway 8. That highway is a symbol of the world Carl and Ruth Henrikson have almost left behind.

They have come—both in their 86th year—full circle, back to live in their hometown.

There is nothing to suggest that out there on the curves of that circle, Carl and Ruth Henrikson profoundly changed the American way of life.

A low profile of modesty, they both say, is the best way to get along in any small town where you grew up and where you have returned to live out your lives.

So very few of their neighbors know that out there on Elm Street is the Carl Henrikson who pioneered the science of opinion polls that brought the technique to its modern use as a tool for measuring public views on any subject, product or concept.

They do not know that Henrikson was a formidable advertising and economic giant along Fifth and Park avenues in New York City for years, organizing a research firm that absorbed the Crosley Poll, paralleling the Gallup Poll; more than 3,400 Crosley pollsters guided product development for everything from peanuts and cereals to automobiles and stoves, clothes and toiletries from the late 1940s into the '60s.

They are not aware that he served as assistant secretary of commerce during World War II and was economic adviser to Harry Truman when he was a Missouri senator.

Nor will the average Lindstrom resident know that in the 1930s, Henrikson was a distinguished educator at the University of Chicago, serving as assistant dean of the school of business. He will only casually mention that he also has been a consultant on marketing and polling sciences for European firms.

Some may have seen his color motion picture of the last logging drive in Minnesota, which now is in the Minnesota State Historical Society library for loan. He won an honorable mention from the Academy of Motion Picture Arts and Sciences for that. "I made the whole film in the 1930s, based on my earlier days at a lumberjack camp, using a cheap camera I bought in Chicago," Henrikson said.

Over to Ruth now, who sits by his side, smiling at his account, waiting patiently to get in a few words.

She is the same Ruth Henrikson who was a member of the Teaneck, N.J., Board of Education on May 13, 1964, when she and six other members of the nine-member board were the first in the United States to vote for voluntary integration of a public school system.

She still remembers that "scary night when opponents stormed the stage where the board sat and how it took police guards to calm things down. And I just sat there until I was alone, wondering what we had done for democracy. Well, we found out, didn't we?"

As she speaks, Ruth holds a book written on the subject and about that night in May.

It all began for Carl and Ruth when they were 15 and students at old Lindstrom High School. Carl has preserved that long-demolished building in one of his oil paintings.

"You sat at double desks then, and Ruth and another girl sat together next to me and another boy. The girl with Ruth handed me a pencil and asked me to sharpen it with my pencil sharpener," says Carl.

"If you do, I'll give you my friend Ruth as your girlfriend," she told Carl. And she did.

After high school, Ruth went off to college; Carl was mustered into duty with the Lindstrom Naval Reserve Militia, first to be called up when America entered World War I.

Ruth became one of the first women to coach basketball in Minnesota, first at Lindstrom and later at Forest Lake. They hired her to teach third grade. She said she didn't know anything about third grade. But they said that was all right because they really wanted her to coach.

Carl's career began as a YMCA worker, which took him to Duluth, which took him into the woods as a lumberjack to earn money for college, which turned out to be two colleges—Williams College in Chicago training YMCA staffers, and the University of Chicago, three blocks away.

Carl married Ruth in 1924 and took her to Chicago and got her a job as typist and switchboard operator at Williams College.

After getting his degree from the University of Chicago, Carl worked as a stockbroker. Later he joined the faculty at the University of Chicago and became one of its economic whizzes and assistant dean of the business school.

"When I left to go to New York City in 1937 and work at the National Association of Credit Men, guess who succeeded me at Chicago? Secretary of State George Shulz," Carl said.

Washington wanted him in World War II, both as a lieutenant commander in the Navy Reserve and in the Commerce Department.

The Commerce Department won.

World War II's end took Carl back to New York City as director of research for J.M. Mathes advertising agency. That led to the Crosley Poll.

"Crosley was an old-timer in the business. We did everything except conduct political polls," Carl says.

"But, yes, what we did in the late 1940s and '50s and early '60s created the science of today. No doubt. I don't want to sound immodest, but sure, I was a big part of it. We tried to bring science into polling."

"And I was back in Teaneck, N.J., raising two children, our son and daughter," says Ruth. "Carl was gone so much I began to get into community work. I guess that led to the notion of running for the board of education."

She was elected to five terms and was the only woman on the board. Carl left Manhattan in 1964 and decided to "retire all the way" in 1973.
(December 16, 1985.)

Storytelling windows have tale of their own

Shakopee. The visitor at St. Mark's Catholic Church admired the exquisite Gothic carved butternut wood center and side altars, and he was properly impressed to know that this church's foundations, put up in 1858, once had been the beginnings of St. John's Abbey, now in Collegeville.

The lofty spires reaching skyward over the town had drawn his attention.

Then his gaze turned to the 13 stained glass windows, 10 of which relate a story of the Gospel. He was awed by them. The rich colors, the art work, the figures are almost Italian Renaissance.

And they tell more than a story of the Gospel. It is a remarkable and strange story, a little known tale of old Vienna, and the fading glory days of the Austro-Hungarian Empire is reflected in each one.

And if the organist on Sundays occasionally lapses into a touch of Viennese composers, Mozart or Bruckner, you can understand when I tell you the story.

There are two characters in the drama:

A young medical student named Mathias Savs, who was destined to become a revered pastor of St. Mark's.

The Emperor Franz Josef, next-to-last ruling monarch of the Austro-Hungarian Empire, symbol of the Golden Age of European civilization before it crumbled in World War I.

Mathias was born in Breg, Austria, in 1870, studied the classics at Innsbruck and entered medical school at the University of Vienna. To finance his studies and also to savor some of the Viennese life in three-quarter time, young Savs was appointed to tutor some of the ancient Hapsburg royal family.

He tutored the youngsters in apartments of the Hofburg winter palace in the Inner Ring and Schonbrunn summer palace on the edge of the city. He learned that the aging emperor was contemplating building a private chapel and had commissioned glassmakers to recreate 10 episodes from the Gospel.

Young Savs may have even seen some of the windows completed before he left the service of the emperor in 1890.

That year Mathias Savs attended a meeting called to hear a young priest named F. X. Bajex, of St. Paul, paint colorful pictures of Minnesota.

Bajex has been sent to Europe by Archbishop John Ireland to recruit novices for the St. Paul Seminary.

Savs liked what he heard. He abandoned his medical studies and followed this unusual Pied Piper of the religious life to Cretin and Summit avenues, where he was ordained in 1895. Just before his death in 1917, Archbishop Ireland appointed the young, gentle priest as dean and "irremovable" rector of St. Mark's in Shakopee.

In 1914, just as World War I began thundering across Europe, Father Savs made a visit to his beloved Vienna. He recalled the stained glass windows and discovered that Franz Josef had abandoned his plans for the chapel. What about the windows?

Father Savs began negotiating to buy them for another Minnesota church that he was serving. But before the windows could be packed and shipped, the war swept aside all such efforts, and the windows were hastily buried in a secret cache.

It wasn't until 1922 that the 10 windows finally arrived in Shakopee—at a cost of $250 each.

To fill in some additional window space, Father Savs commissioned the same Viennese firm to execute three more windows, one of them a World War I memorial dedicated to the men and women from St. Mark's who served.

The original 10 depict the Immaculate Conception, Nativity, Mary Magdalene annointing Jesus' feet, St.

Dominic receiving the rosary, the Apparition of the Sacred Heart, the Holy Family, St. Anthony's bread, the Prodigal Son, Christ blessing the children, the Guardian Angel, and Pentecost.

Sav's beautiful windows, with their cobalt blues, pinks, shadows of gray and vivid reds and oranges and yellows, have added a visual dimension to worship at St. Mark's for 62 years. They are framed against the backdrop of the altars made by woodmaster F. X. Hirscher, who also did the altar in St. Paul's Assumption Catholic Church.
(September 21, 1984.)

Barber has seen long and short of it

Emmons. Chances are that if you are boy or man and live anywhere within 50 miles of this town on the Minnesota-Iowa border, you'll drop into Gordon "Sharkey" Lee's Old Reliable barber shop, pool hall and candy store sometime between now and Christmas for your annual holiday tonsorial splurge.

That would follow the pattern of your grandfather and father.

When Sharkey stuck that Old Reliable sign on the front window in November 1920, he meant just what it says.

The other day he celebrated 65 years in the same shop and was revving up for his 87th birthday and dusting off the sign that says: No loitering in the barber chair.

And Sharkey can cut hair and shave as deftly with or without glasses.

"Some customers sort of like to have me wear glasses, as a protective measure," he said.

The price of a haircut is $3 (kids under 14 get it for
$2.75) and a shave is $2. And if you want the "works" with
lotion, it's $6.50.

The fringe benefits include Sharkey's 65 years worth of
barbering philosophies, which have earned him the roles as
legend, personality and sage in a tiny community of eccentric character, where most residents spend half their days in
Minnesota and the rest in Iowa, just a step across the main
street.

"I would guess that I have worked on 200,000 heads and
faces," said Sharkey when I chanced into his shop one
recent Thursday night.

I happened to be in the vicinity because I was invited to
speak, and everybody shouldn't go home without stopping
in to see Sharkey.

"At 9 at night?"

"Well, I like to be accommodating for the farmers and
city folk who work all day in Albert Lea or Austin, so I gen-
erally open about 7:30 a.m. and close about 11 p.m.," he
said as he finished a deluxe job on Selmer "Sally" Soren-
son's hair. Sally cautioned Sharkey to do a good job
because, "I'm going out on the town at the Legion Club
next door and might meet a movie starlet."

"Actually," said Sharkey, who has seen the long and the
short of things in the barber business, "we don't have an
athletic club or private club or community center and social
center in town, except for the Legion Club next door and
Buttermaker's supper club. So I sort of keep this place and
the pool tables and candy counter for folks to drop in and
just while away the time while we solve the world's problems and think up a few new ones."

Of course you can reserve your time, too, as many former customers do who live in St. Paul, Des Moines and Minneapolis.

Hair styles for men are getting shorter these days, Sharkey said, and he spurs that fashion on with a sign that urges men with long hair to throw away their hair driers and get a real hair styling with a 60-year-old steel razor, sharpened on a 100-year-old Swatty hone, stropped on a 75-year-old strop, shiny from wear.

In an era when few men get shaved in shops, most of Sharkey's estimated 12 daily customers get shaved because they like to feel the lather going on, cool and aromatic with the big old-fashioned brush, which mixes the lather in a big, old-fashioned mug from water in a big, old-fashioned round sink.

"It's a production," Kenny Rasmusson told Sharkey the other day, when the barber worked on his nearly baldpate so "he'd look good in the beauty contest he's entering next week."

"The men and boys in this town know they are part of history when they sit in his chair and get their ears lowered," said Marilyn Flugum, the effervescent Emmons reporter for a network of area newspapers, who organized Sharkey's 65th-anniversary party with a big dinner at the Legion Club. Two hundred people showed up, including a TV reporter. "I've been getting letters and calls from all over the Midwest from people who saw it," Sharkey said.

One of the questions the TV reporter asked bachelor Sharkey is when he plans to retire.

"Haven't got time," he snapped.

But he is used to international fame radiating from his shop.

A few years ago, Albert Lea artist Lloyd Herfindahl, who was born in Emmons, came down and painted Sharkey cutting hair. He took the painting to Paris for an art show, and some gallery has been circulating it in a traveling exhibit around Europe.

"I was up in Minneapolis the other day and met a Norwegian like myself who had been in Madrid," said Sharkey. "And he said: 'You look familiar. I have seen your face somewhere just lately.' I asked where he had been. He said Madrid. I said I'd never been much beyond the Iowa line. Then the man said: 'That's where I saw your picture. In Madrid. In a painting in an art gallery show. You were cutting hair.'"

"Whatta you know?" said Sharkey, "Maybe some day I'll be cutting hair on a wall in the Louvre."
(December 16, 1985.)

This is placid Red Wing?

Red Wing. As you go down the highways and biways of Minnesota this summer, don't forget the St. James Hotel-Mall complex here in pretty Red Wing.

The map says you are in Red Wing, corner of Bush and Main, in a quiet, placid, lazy setting. Then what are all those tour buses doing there? And the platoons of tourists? They seem to be going in and out of the old St. James Hotel as if it were a beehive.

Let's go see the honey.

You walk through the Victorian glass paneled doors into a covered village of shop fronts, a big carpeted "village plaza," with a doorway leading into the restored St. James hotel lobby, classically and fashionably showing its original late 19th century elegance. Save that for later.

It was lunchtime and for that I chose the cavernous stone Port of Red Wing subterranean restaurant. It's long on stone arches, with good, but not great, cuisine.

I had a second choice that day, the Veranda Coffee shop which had been open less than a week. It is ringed by glass windows overlooking the riverfront and on days like these the doors open out onto the patio for dining at tables with umbrellas (or sans umbrellas for sun tanning). You can have breakfast, or lunch on soups, salads, omelettes, baked beans, Wisconsin bratwurst and cole slaw.

There is an incredible view, too, just as you enter the Steamboat Park Gallery on the mezzanine mall level. Your gaze sweeps up and up and up and up for five floors of atrium, one wall of which is covered with a two-story mural of old Red Wing scenes. It is the largest painting I have seen since Titian's giants in Venice. This is no Titian. It was painted by J.T. Butch, the scenery designer at Chanhassen Dinner Theater. It is mind-boggling.

The gallery offers a selection of works—long on landscapes—by Red Wing area artists. Their names are not necessarily on every art buff's lips, but you may shortly hear more about James Zotalis, Don Marco the color crayonist, Larry Veeder and Herb Hultgren. Also John Runions, the Alma, Wis., painter and batik stylist Carol Martin of Rochester, the latter two well-established.

So is the Steamboat Gallery since it weighed anchor last fall.

The Chanhassen connection?

Simple. The entire St. James Hotel-Village Mall and office building rising over much of it came from the creative minds of Chanhassen Dinner Theater owner Herb Bloomberg and his wife, Carol, interior design artist, who turned what suddenly seemed to be a lot of pipe dreams into what suddenly seems to make sense to downtown Red Wing.

And also the Red Wing Shoe Co., which primed the financial pump for the project plus Citizen Security Insurance Co., whose home offices now occupy most of the five floors of the addition.

Hot or cold, muggy, or sub-zero, storming or blizzarding, the St. James Hotel-Mall is all-weather and one can live rather opulently without ever venturing outside.

Ride the elevators fronting on the mall plaza to the fifth floor and you step off under a recessed ceiling of ornate stained glass, with an immense and lavishly trimmed copper chandelier hanging from the center.

You are now in what soon will be the cherry-on-the-whipped cream topping—the Hiawatha Valley rooftop dining and cocktail lounge, already being used for catered private parties and dinners. The entire setting is enclosed by floor to ceiling windows, facing three views of the river and the city.

Back once more on the mall, you browse, and sometimes buy from, apparel shops of class and fashion; meander through the bookshop, Hobby Hutch, and are tempted to sin in Darveaux's Confectionaire, where I watched enviously as tourists vacuumed up varieties of chocolate barks, candy bars, wedges of candy, all hand-made, mostly chocolate with nuts, fillings.

"Aw, come on, try a sample," said the sales person.

"No," I said. "I must be brave."

I felt noble all the way into the hotel lobby, where a young woman was playing piano sonatas on a baby grand piano and the graciousness of the interior's charm made me wish I could stay and take one of the 24 rooms which are all restored.

"A good thing it is only a wish. We're booked solid through the weekend," said the desk clerk.
(June 17, 1980.)

Courthouse doubles as art museum

Albert Lea. A functioning courthouse—and an art museum? What is happening to the 98-year-old Freeborn County Courthouse was almost a matter of missing the forest for the trees.

"We were sitting around at a meeting of the Freeborn County Arts Committee one morning a year and a half ago," says Clifford Lund.

"The subject was creating a major art museum in town to supplement what we already have to project our visibility as the gateway to Minnesota for tourism."

The minutes will show that it was Ray Hemenway, grand old man of DFL politics and an artist himself, who said:

"Gentlemen, have you ever taken a long, hard look at the building we're in? At the ornate façade with its carved sculptures? At the Italian ceramic floor scuffed by maybe a million feet, the still-beautiful marble fireplaces in almost every office? And I see all those empty walls that beg to be covered with art."

District Court Judge James Mork, another committee person, who presides in the turn-of-the century courtroom of "real character," says now that the lights went on in every member's head almost simultaneously.

Blessings from the County Board and enthusiasm from a lot of office staff and administrators have turned an idea into reality.

"What we have rediscovered is the architectural beauty of a building that serves as a sort of picture frame for what we're adding little by little," says Albert Lea artist Lloyd Herfindahl, head of the committee's art acquisitions.

"The building itself is a museum. It ranks as one of the most venerable and beautifully executed governmental citadels in the state," he said.

"We went out that day of decision and really scrutinized something we'd all taken for granted, something so familiar we never really looked at it as anything but the old courthouse," says member Joanne Barr.

They suddenly saw the gargoyles—the two shaggy-eared dogs framed over one of the big Romanesque arches; the heads of a man and woman over another; the cleaned red stone and brick; the mere suggestion of the minaret towers and bell and clock tower that once rose high off the Broadway hill against the prairie skyline.

Last spring, the first original work, a large mural telling the history of Freeborn County, was unveiled and hung on a wall on the landing between the first- and second-floor staircase, itself a woodcarver's gem.

The work was done by Herfindahl, who also recently completed two more depicting the history of the judicial system. These were hung in the courtroom—with great ceremony—in early November. Speakers included retired U.S. Judge Miles Lord and State Historical Society director Russell Fridley.

Waiting to be hung are 15 print etchings by former Albert Lea artist Mary Kelly, who lives in London. The same prints are in a collection in London's Tate Gallery.

The arts committee also has acquired a major work by Albert Lea native Scott Troe, who now lives in the Lofoten Islands off the Norwegian coast and recently visited Albert Lea with an exhibit of his oil landscapes of Norway.

He is one of Norway's most salable and popular artists.

"We are trying to assemble a good collection of Minnesota's good artists," says Lund, whose private collection of Cameron Booth, Elof Wedin and Adolf Dehn is among the best in the state.

In the offing are efforts to acquire sculpture by Paul Granlund and Peter Lupori.

And also a LeRoy Neiman original.

"This," says Lund, "is just the start."

The reaction of the people who work in the Freeborn County Courthouse to the new museum concept has been enthusiastic. Employees have dusted off old paintings and prints of their own to hang and some hitherto unknown etchings and prints of the original courthouse have surfaced.

Select employees are being trained as tour guides, not only for the art work, but also the building.

"You know, almost everybody in the county comes through this building at least once or twice a year for licenses, to pay taxes, appear in court. What better and more democratic place for an art museum," says Herfindahl.

To divert tourists off I-35 from the south, the committee is designing an art brochure, pinpointing Albert Lea galleries, museums and architectural landmarks for distribution at the Minnesota information center where I-35 enters from Iowa.

Says Lund:

"What we want to do is establish Albert Lea as the art gateway to Minnesota from the south and say, 'Look, this is just a brief look and preview at what's waiting for you up in the big art centers of the Twin Cities and Duluth.'"

To think that 15 years ago the courthouse was almost demolished.

(January 3, 1986.)

Echos of past grace Cedarhurst

Cottage Grove. Sometimes on still summer evenings, you can almost hear their voices echoing out of the past.

Presidents Teddy Roosevelt, William Howard Taft, Warren G. Harding and Queen Marie of Romania. Frank B. Kellogg is sitting at a desk in the library, drafting the ill-fated Kellogg-Briand Peace Pact of 1928, talking about it with Cordenio Severance, his law partner and host.

The women are in the garden, lighted by coach lamps, the voice of Mary Severance coming through as gracious hostess.

"Our guests and visitors who come here are enthralled by the thought that such distinguished people have used these rooms, sat at these tables and on these chairs and admired the lawns and gardens," says Ron Nienaber, who with his wife Jean, is celebrating the fifth anniversary as owner of Cedarhurst mansion in rural Cottage Grove.

It's "Cedarhurst's third barony," as someone has called this period in referring to the three major episodes in its life.

Not at all in the guise of a baron, Ron was busy painting the summer house near the entrance driveway. Jean was deep in the culinary recesses, making ready the night's monthly International Dinner Tour.

It would be a German-Austrian meal of six courses, with filet of sole and stuffed pork chops, Viennese style; caraway potatoes, dangerously rich Prince Regent torte.

Guests would assemble and stroll in the garden, sit at umbrellaed tables on the rear porch-patio, then dine in the grand ballroom, listening to Mary Neal play on the mighty 18-rank Wurlitzer organ. After which Ron would lead the tour of many of the 26 rooms, all but that wing and area reserved for the "Baron and the Baroness."

"Which is us," he laughs.

Something new had been added to the walls of the dining room and library since my last visit to Cedarhurst: oil portraits by Howard Chandler Christy of Cordenio Severance and a matching portrait of Mary by S. Seymour Thomas, a lesser-known, but accomplished portrait painter.

"'We got them just six months ago. Can I tell you the story?" asks Jean. "One day a few years ago a man visited for one of our lunches or dinners, maybe a wedding reception. Anyway, he knew there had been these two paintings at the Science Museum in the old Gov. Merriam mansion behind the State Capitol. He helped Ron trace them to the vaults of the Minneapolis Art Institute. They offered to let us have them on permanent loan and we lucked out. A descendant of the Severance family donated the money for their restoration and frames."

It is the first time the portraits have ever hung in the mansion.

The Nienabers think it is apropos that the original owners of Cedarhurst now peer down with expressions of gracious benevolence at life in the mansion à la 1983 because "we always consider them to be the real host and hostess of Cedarhurst if you will, and those of us who came later are merely proprietors and custodians of that past," says Jean.

The original portion of the mansion was built about 1860 by Mary Severance's maternal grandfather, Charles O.

Fanning. In 1888 and again in 1917, the mansion was remodeled and expanded, so that now it has twin Grecian revival pillared porticos, a wide veranda with ornamental pilaster railing and a long wall of French windows, fronting sweeping lawns and flower beds, cloistered from the Washington County Road 19 traffic by tall hedgerows.

Mary was the daughter of Civil War Gen. Samuel Harriman and came to live at Cedarhurst as a child. She was a graduate of Carleton College, and Severance Hall dormitory there is named for her.

Cordenio came out of Mantorville, the same place Frank B. Kellogg had practiced law. They were friends and law partners in St. Paul. When Kellogg was elected to the U.S. Senate, Severance offered Cedarhurst as a focus of social and formal gatherings. Thus came the world's great names by train to Cedarhurst in the early quarter of the century. Often their special and private Pullman cars would be parked at Newport siding and the VIPs—kings, queens, diplomats, ambassadors and presidents—were driven a dusty seven miles to the seclusion of the mansion behind the tall pine rows. They rode in caravans of limousines, often with Secret Service men riding the running boards.

Then it was that the ballroom rang with music, dancing feet, sparkling conversation. Sumptuous meals—Jean Nienaber has revived that tradition—were served and guests roamed the several dozen acres, on which much of the food had been grown.

Kellogg's role as secretary of state and ambassador to the Court of St. James enhanced the prestige of Cedarhurst and there are clippings claiming that the Kellogg-Briand Peace Pact renouncing war took shape in the library.

The curtain fell on all that pageantry in the 1930s. Both Severances had died four years before the Peace Pact was signed in 1929. The stage was fairly bare and barely visible until U.S. Army Col. Francis A. Markoe bought Cedarhurst at the end of World War II and moved his large family of seven sons into it. The colonel, a St. Paul native and West Point graduate, had served with classmates Dwight Eisenhower, Walter Bedell Smith and Mark Clark. He lived at Cedarhurst as a self-proclaimed "gentleman farmer," but he also worked for the CIA and his old friend Bedell Smith, its first director. Cedarhurst's "Second Empire" under Markoe enjoyed another era of romance and intrigue. It is said that many distinguished diplomats and statesmen from behind the Iron Curtain used Cedarhurst as a way station in their flight to freedom.

Alas, Cedarhurst sagged again into dishevelment when the Markoes departed in the 1960s, and rescue by the Nienabers came just in the nick of time, "although there have been days of leaky roofs and other structural problems when we haven't been sure."

The Nienabers have recreated their version of Cedarhurst's traditional hospitality as a tourist attraction, with scheduled tours, including lunches and dinners, wedding receptions, testimonial parties and community theater.

"And we always invite the ghosts of the past to join us," says Ron.

(June 17, 1983.)

Invitation a sign St. Paul, St. Peter
brothers again

St. Peter. St. Paul Mayor George Latimer is going to St. Peter this month to mend a fence that has been broken for 127 years.

That was the time—in 1857—when Joe Rolette, son of a French-Canadian fur trader, a man of robust humor who loved to dress like an Indian or voyageur, stole the bill the Territorial Legislature had approved that would have moved the capital of the pending new state of Minnesota from St. Paul to St. Peter.

The rift, if not anger and disappointment, that followed has been a bone of contention all these years.

Until now, no St Paul official has ever been invited to appear or speak in St. Peter. Latimer will be the first. He will speak to the St. Peter Area Chamber of Commerce at its annual meeting Jan. 31.

This proferring of the olive branch was done through the good offices of Bob Wettergren, the St. Peter area group's longtime manager, a descendant of a pioneer St. Peter family and affectionately known as "Mr. St. Peter."

He and I have formed a warm friendship over the years that has transcended this official cleavage between the two cities. And so when I heard about Latimer's mission, I got in touch with Wettergren.

He readily took the credit, or blame ("who knows how much deep-seated animosity will manifest itself that evening from die-hards?") for this attempt at burying the hatchet, or as such loyal St. Peterites as historian Marjorie Schmidt put it, "Forgive a sinner and right a wrong."

Wettergren says that he got this brainstorm during a conversation at the last of five area Swedish-Norwegian lutefisk church dinners he attended during the Christmas season.

"This one was at the Scandian Grove Swedish Lutheran Church," he says, "and food and conviviality like that wash warm waves of euphoria and feelings of peace and good will over everybody. I mentioned I was looking for a speaker at our annual dinner, and someone suggested Mayor Latimer and said it was time we let bygones be bygones."

Wettergren agrees, of course, that the loss of the capital for St. Peter may not have been all Joe Rolette's fault. He could have been merely the agent in a plot hatched by a group of patriotic friends, a slightly brash, political and civic faction dedicated to saving the capital for St. Paul.

The story, of course, is that a vast majority of the territorial legislators from the rural areas decided that when it came time for statehood, the capital certainly shouldn't be located in St. Paul. It had a poor location, so far east, so far from the western and northern boundaries of the state. A number of sites were proposed. One, even more logical, was a piece of land near Kandiyohi, ideally situated in the center of the state.

But St. Peter got a bigger vote.

The bill was adopted and was on its way to the governor when it reached Rolette, a legislator from Pembina (now in North Dakota). Rolette was chairman of the enrollment committee, and was supposed to give it his imprimatur and pass it to the governor.

There are several versions of what happened next. Ramsey County historian Virginia Brainard Kunz, in her research, has decided that Rolette pocketed the bill, walked over to Truman and Smith's bank and locked it in a vault.

Then he switched hotels and went into hiding until the session ended.

One story is that Rolette appeared dramatically at the last moment, flashing the bill, knowing it was too late for the governor's signature.

When he appeared at the last moment in dramatic fashion, it was too late to get any more bills signed. Later efforts to amend that diabolical practical joke, if it was one, were to no avail. Whether Joe acted alone, venting his strange sense of humor, or acted in concert with others is not clear.

Poor St. Peter. It had created wide avenues and prepared fine, sturdy buildings, including a potential capitol building. It named its main street Minnesota Avenue. It was prepared to welcome the prosperity and growth of a state capital town. Instead, it got the Nicollet County courthouse and jail.

Nothing ever came of future attempts to move the capital.

But to borrow an old saying, St. Peterites seemed to believe that if you can't move the mountain, you can send Mohammed to it. St. Peter managed to provide Minnesota with five governors—Willis Gorman, Henry Swift, Horace Austin, Andrew McGill and John A. Johnson.

Rolette lived out his years and is buried in the Catholic cemetery in Prairie du Chien, Wis. He is enshrined with an oil portrait in full voyageur's regalia hanging on the landing between the foyer and first floor of the Minnesota Club, where annual toasts are drunk by St. Paul loyalists to his dubious courage, guile and audacity.

Wettergren says that Mayor Latimer has assured him he is bringing felicitations, greetings and perhaps even a few postcards of the City Hall Indian God of Peace, appropriately, to the chamber meeting.

"We're going to give him every chance to establish detente," says Wettergren. "I've invited him to tell the St. Paul version of what happened on my TV show; there will be a big reception in the American Legion Club and then the dinner in the VFW Hall. This is a night when we play no favorites."

One thing bothers Wettergren a bit.

"George and Joe look a lot alike," he says. "Put a voyageur's outfit on George and you'd think Joe Rolette had been reincarnated."

(January 6, 1984.)

A visit to Bavaria by way of Stillwater . . .

Stillwater. These are days and nights for stay-at-homes when it is fun to travel vicariously and plan...

By evening, almost a half foot of snow had fallen, turning the pines and the eaves of the Bavarian-style chalet into a picture postcard of an Alpine inn. Lights glow warmly from windows.

It was a Friday night and the annual meeting of the Bavarian Verein (Club) in Karl and Denise Schoene's Gasthaus Bayerische Jaeger (Gasthaus Bavarian Hunter), just west of Stillwater, off County Road 15.

The snow fell in big flakes and the air smelled clean and fresh and fragrant of pines. Just beyond the front door in the Tiergarten, the deer frolicked and the big white rabbits blended against the snowscape.

Aromas of wienerschnitzel, sauerbraten, rotkohl (red cabbage) and kartoffel knoedel (potato dumplings) poured out of the open door. Zither music wafted through the room and then came the music of the accordion player Phil Nelles ambling from room to room.

Already the two big dining rooms were filled and we went to our Stammtisch (family table) near the porcelain Nurnberg stove in the Bayernstube (country room).

Here came the Pfannkuchs, Olaf and Georgette; and Der Reise Buro Chef (travel agency director) John Bekkering of Atmos, new wife, Gloria, and his mother Frau Cornelia Bekkering of Venverboc, Holland. Gerry Oshea joined us and Der Herr Ober (Karl Schoene) hovered when he could.

And Frau Kurt Erben wheeled in and out with the dishes and the tall mugs of foaming beer, the glasses of wine from the Mosel and the Rheinfalz and Rheingau, the Rudesheimer and the Ingleheimer Rot (red).

Outside was Minnesota and snow and winter, but inside was a little Gasthof near Reit-im-Winkl in the foothills of the Alps near Bernau and Herrenchiemsee.

The room was filled with toasts "Zum Wohls" and "Prosits." And Frau Erben arrived with platters of Vorspeise—wurst, celery root salad, North Sea herring in tomato-mustard sauce, kaese (cheese) and two kinds of dark, German bread.

Then came the leber knoedel suppe (liver dumpling soup) and another round of Schorrbrau from Muenchen (Munich) and the conversation at the table roamed from Mme. Pfannkuch's French to Frau Bekkering's Dutch and Olaf Pfannkuch's "Aachen" accented German. And Karl's "Landshuetter" Deutsch.

Mr. Oshea managed a few words of Gaelic.

Kalsbshaxe (veal knuckle) for me, and red cabbage; Jaeger schnitzel for Frau Bekkering and Leberkaese for John and Gloria and across the table schnitzels and sauerbratens.

Warmth flowed across us and the adjoining tables and we were far away from wherever we had been that day. For most of us had experiences in similar German gasthofs to recount.

Then, as the evening peaked, we adjourned to the down-stairs Weinstube for the meeting and slides of past Bavarian Club tours and talk of this year's to come. And Reise Buro Chef Bekkering passed out this season's schedule of Condor charters from the Twin Cities to Frankfurt and return.

And this year something new in Frankfurt—an Atmos Agency office to assist travelers at the German end of the trip.

Retired St. Paul banker Warren Heintz, who once brought German know-how to Scandinavian Payne Avenue, confided he had just finished making his first vio-lin—a retirement hobby.

The tenth annual meeting of the Bayerische Verein ended with bartender Kurt Erben drawing beer and pouring wine for a round.

There was a reluctance to leave, to travel those thou-sands of miles through mental pathways back home on a snowy, cold Friday night.

Nobody did before some German lieder had been sung, Schrammel music played and somewhere from upstairs came music and voices and sounds of "Schunkeling"—people linking arms and swaying in a chain, back and forth.

"Aufwiedersehen!" carried across the snowy pines of the Kurpark and Wienerwald Germany lay back there in the glow of the rear car window.

It is last Sunday afternoon, 3:30 p.m. Thirty or more of us are sitting in chairs in the once grand ballroom on the third floor of 30 Crocus Place, Hill district, spectacular view of the city. Afternoon sort of burnt umber in the snow, mist across the Mississippi Valley.

We sit in front of a screen in a home once owned by Louis Hill, Jr., grandson of Empire Builder James J. Hill. Now, it is the residence of Dr. Matt and Ann Walton, he the head of the geological survey in Minnesota, she an art connoisseur of Europe, especially France.

On the screen flashes—not the Super Bowl, but a "Voyage through France, off the beaten path," as created for a summer roaming by Madame Georgette Pfannkuch (here she is again) and her husband Olaf (here he is again) of the University of Minnesota geology department.

For an hour or so, while the Dallas Cowboys get roped by the Pittsburgh Steelers, we wander via slides through 34,000 years of civilization, along the highways from Paris to Fontainebleau, through Bourges, Clermont-Ferrand, Auvergne, Le Puy, Roquefort for the cheeses, also St. Nectaire for the cheeses, tasting wines in the vineyards and wineries of Sancerrois.

This is southern France, where you seldom meet an American and where the ancestors of Georgette lived, an area in the Massif Central (plateau of south central France) and where all the periods of European culture are fastened layer upon layer.

Here in the little villages are wines, foods seldom tasted by tourists.

But they will be by some 30 pilgrims who will venture forth in June.

(January 26, 1979.)

Auld Lang Syne was best
when sung at Beyer's hotel

New Ulm. New Year's Eve is for reminiscing. Lost Spur club manager Harry "Hucky" Beyer, Jr. had that in mind when he spread out the March 31, 1939 *New Ulm Daily Journal* on the lunch table.

That was the day, 41 years ago, when Hucky's father, Harry Sr., two uncles, Al and Herb, and Grandpa August Beyer were feted by Hucky's and my hometown. The occasion was the 25th anniversary of Beyer's hotel, a legendary hostelry, dining center and bar-with-dancing that lined the railroad mainlines during the first half of the century.

Hucky stabbed a finger at a column called "Hitting the Hi Spots," which I wrote when I was 17-going-on-18, and sports editor of the *Journal.*

For all the time until Hucky left for the Twin Cities, we celebrated New Year's Eve in New Ulm at two places—at the Turner Hall Club up on the hill and at the Beyer's hotel across the tracks in Goosetown.

But, as Hucky says, every eve was New Year's Eve at Beyer's, called the Northwestern until 1938 because it was directly across from the Chicago & North Western depot. Every day "drummers" (traveling salesmen) and passengers came and went from the four first-class passenger trains that came from Chicago on the east and Rapid City on the west. Those were the days when everybody still traveled by train.

The hotel had three stories with an L shaped wood frame stuccoed over it in a pale yellow. It rose off the skyline like a skyscraper, complementing the huge globular elevators of the nearby Eagle Roller flour mill.

It was Grandma Beyer's cooking that lured the traveling salesmen from their Pullmans and club cars across the tracks, their sample cases fresh from the wholesale houses of Chicago, St. Paul and Mankato. They spewed forth to fill Grandma Beyer's 27 immaculate rooms, some with bath.

Downstairs, you always could get a drink, even in the dry years and the frivolity of the old fashioned country bar spread naturally into the adjoining dining rooms. There "Country New Ulm German home-cooking" was served, plus steaks decorated by hashed browns, herring or head cheese appetizers, and slices of half dollar-sized home-cured sausages.

August Beyer had come from Pommern, Germany, and originally settled in nearby Courtland, where he and his wife ran a small saloon-hotel-café. In 1914, when they bought the Northwestern and migrated to the city they brought their own brand of hospitality, including Grandma Beyer's style of cooking. Before she died in 1929 she passed on her recipes to the sons.

What I remember about the cooking was the quantity. Except for the 18-ounce T-bones and porterhouses and the 16-ounce New York strip steaks (at $3 even into the late 1950s) everything was served family style. Platters of pork chops with onion-cream gravy, roast beef or veal cutlets and sometimes ham were replenished when empty as long as diners wanted more.

On weekend nights, Fezz Fritsche would bring his Goosetown polka band around to play and it was there, in the late 1940s, that his famous "Tanta Anna" polka was premiered and became a Top 40 Golden Record within months.

During the terrible Armistice Day blizzard of 1940, when four passenger trains were stalled near the depot, everybody waded through the drifts to Beyer's and stayed two days. They probably were as comfortable, well fed and lubricated as any storm victims on record. In fact, even when the blizzard ended, some didn't want to leave.

Beyer's hotel still stands. But its namesakes have long departed—Al, Harry Sr. and Herb have died, Hucky is seeking his second fortune in the Twin Cities. He is still involved in ownership of the building.

Not even an echo of the last passenger train whistle sounds on this New Year's Eve. The salesmen drive cars and stay in those squat-roofed motels up on the highway. And they eat their New Year's Eve dinner in fast-food restaurants.

(December 31, 1980.)

Driving into the past

New Trier. There was a half tank of gasoline in the car and a half day to spend. We decided to go exploring for little villages you see as small dots and names on a map, but just never visit.

At noon on a perfect May day we headed south on U.S. 52 to the State highway 50 exit just south of Hampton and drove east three miles until the landmark tower of St. Mary's Catholic Church came out of the dusty haze, marking New Trier.

Far from its namesake city on the Mosel in Germany, New Trier lay still and bright in a warm, almost hot noon day sun.

The grandiose red brick, white columned church sat regally, looking down on the village from its throne on

"Mary's Hill." The church dwarfs the other buildings, of the community—population 153.

It was lunchtime and there are two good choices in New Trier, tourist attractions ranking with the church.

There is the Trophy House or Dan's, restaurant-night clubs, both busy at lunch, populated by delivery and service people, families, farmers and businessmen. We chose Dan's, because we knew about its salad bar which, at $2.50 offers a luscious variety of icy salads. ranging from tuna or shrimp through potato and slaws, herring and fresh vegetables.

We shared a thick Reuben, grilled on the spot by hostess-chef Jean Hartung, wife of owner Dan. Washed down with a frosty, foaming lager from the tap, this was a good beginning for the afternoon's meander.

The Trophy House we would reserve for the prime rib dinner ($6.95) on Saturday nights or the baked chicken and biscuits served Sunday noon.

Julian Tix, one of the last descendants of those 1854 immigrants from Trier, Germany, helped us focus on the history of St. Mary's before we headed that way.

As if someone had advance knowledge of our coming, the sound of children's voices, lifted in song, sifted from the church as we walked up the stairs.

"The school children are practicing for First Communion," a teacher explained.

The present St. Mary's (founded in 1855) was built in 1909, the third church on "Mary Hill," and it was designed after similar edifices in the region of Trier, in Italian renaissance-Teutonic solidarity. Typical of those Rhenish cathedrals is the statue of Mary, holding an infant Jesus, and standing in queenly pose behind glass over the portal.

When she is lighted at night, she can be seen like a beacon of hope for miles around.

The interior was marked by stained glass windows, bearing names of some of those pioneer families. It was dim and cool and there was a sense of being 5,500 miles away, on the banks of the Mosel in some 18th century church.

That spell continued into the churchyard, where names on the monuments of Tix, Fuchs, Conzemius, Siebernaler marked the heritage of the village....

"Hier ruht in Frieden" (Here rest in peace).

We walked over to the schoolhouse, where 56 children in the first six grades fill the rooms on two floors of the 1900 red brick school with its polished, parqueted floors, ornamental balustrade edging the wide staircase.

Had the youngsters come into the halls wearing styles of 80 years ago, it would have been as if time had stood still.

We left New Trier and went east again on No. 50, to the Welch Village turnoff on Goodhue No. 7 and that took us on a roller coaster descent into an enchanted valley, fingering through hills. It bent and turned haphazardly along a bubbling, splashing stream. The blacktop gave way to gravel and our car sent dust puffs in its wake. Each time we stopped to inhale the still air, filled with nature's perfumes, we heard no sound except those of birds and the rustling squirrels.

There were idyllic picnic paradises, one after the other, wild flowers in pastels, vivid blues and pinks, and always the faint echo of water flowing merrily toward the Cannon River somewhere near.

In almost ten miles of driving and pausing, we saw no other human being, no remnant of human habitation, not one empty beer can, trash bag, plastic pop container.

Then, all at once, No. 7 had brought us to Vasa, that
Swedish settlement. Now it is faded into a crossroads lined
with some empty storefronts. But the noble monument of
worship, Vasa Lutheran Church, with its sprawling, rich
green lawns and shade trees, remains for reflection.

The church and the big monument on a hillside are both
an historical connection. This monument is dedicated to
the memory of Dr. Erik Norelius, one of the state's leading
Swedish theologians, writers and educators, founder of Vasa
church and Gustavus Adolphus College in St. Peter. His
descendants continued his publishing work in the Lind-
strom-Chisago City-Center City area.

Dr. Norelius is buried in front of the large marker and
tourists as well as pilgrims find their way to Vasa.

So we fumbled on No. 7 into the afternoon, turning left
on No. 9 and found, at last, the town of Goodhue, named
for the founder of the St. Paul *Pioneer* (*Press*).

It sits in full view on a platter of land, the main street still
retaining a few remnants of Victorian business buildings,
but the eyebrow raiser is the burst of homes built in a sub-
urban attachment that seems optimistic, but somehow out
of the mold of sturdy old houses on tree-shaded streets that
fill the rest of the town.

Someone had told me that Goodhue would yield the best
Mettwurst I had ever tasted. I was directed to Heaney and
Gorman, a flashy, modern new market and found my mettwurst, dispensed by a rather brusque, hurried butcher, who
cared not at all about the fame of his sausage.

A map will suggest a couple of ways to get you back home
without going over old ground. We picked State Highway
58 into Red Wing, running through magnificent and hilly
scenery and Hay Creek, with its small general store-saloon

with outdoor garden tables, reminiscent of those country roadside taverns in Greece.

The Highway 58 route is the long way home, but we enjoyed it and arrived having used five gallons of gas with $15 spent for souvenirs and memorabilia... and with memories of another world in our own backyard.
(May 16, 1980.)

Shoveling away the years

Chisago City. "Well," he said, shaking hands, "I'm still managing to stay out of my old job."

For more than 40 years until he retired at 93, George Noren (also Noreen) was Chisago City's chief grave digger.

Friday he will be 104.

He has never been a patient in a hospital.

He has almost 20-20 eyesight.

He has never smoked or taken a drink he'll admit to.

His diet has defied all the best nutritional standards—he was weaned, nourished and sustained on fried foods, gaseous vegetables like boiled cabbage; sausage, fried eggs, all the fish he could catch in the lakes around his home, bacon, salt pork, as much coffee as he could hold, rutabagas, turnips, parsnips, plenty of bread and butter, pies, cakes.

"Until I got here to the home and now they poach and bake and broil and undercook all the vegetables. I'd sure like to have pair of thick, fried pork chops," he says wistfully.

"Since you were here last (I've recorded his 90th and 100th birthdays) I took my first pill—but I won't repeat that mistake," he chuckled.

"Listen," he says, "I wish people wouldn't keep saying 'George, you will be 104.' When you anticipate something, sometimes it doesn't come true. I'd hate to miss that birthday. I knew a lady in town who was going to be 100 and she kept talking about it and the day before her birthday she got sick and died."

George would still be living in his old home if his second wife, now dead, hadn't become ill ten years ago or so. They moved to the Margaret Parmly Retirement-Nursing home. That's where George has kept his shared one-room with a big picture-window and his big, oversized-oval thermometer just outside.

Ten years ago when the present building was erected, they looked around for someone to turn the first shovelful of dirt.

"Of course they came to me. Who else could dig like me?" said George.

Just to prove it, he points to a picture on the wall showing him turning over a big, big load of dirt with that gold-plated spade.

"You took that picture of me," he said. I remembered. I also remembered the picture I took hanging next to it—of George digging a grave the day after his 90th birthday.

George's eyes twinkled.

"You remember how you called the morning after my 90th and my wife said, 'Oh, he's not here. He's out in the cemetery.' And you said 'I'm sorry to hear that. The party must have been too much for him.' And she said, 'Oh, it was quite a party, all right, but he's not in the cemetery resting. He's working. He's digging a grave."

"And when I was 100," he said, "You caught me shoveling snow out in front here."

George says he is getting a little weaker, though, and doesn't shovel much anymore. Doesn't go out in this icy, snowy weather.

On his 100th birthday, when his relatives put on a huge bash for him, George walked two blocks to nearby Zion Lutheran Church for the party. "This year, we'll have it right here in the home," said his son, Ted, who dropped by to leave an electric razor he'd had repaired for his father.

"This year," said his son, "It won't be so big and lively an affair."

They always get George's birthday mixed into Valentine's Day and make him the King of Hearts at the home.

"You know, he complains about missing the old pork chops and steak and fried potatoes, but he's not wasting away," said Ted.

"I weighed in at 173 pounds the last time," said George. "But that's about five pounds less than when I was 20."

People are always asking him how he happened to live so long and he shakes his head and says:

"I often wonder the same thing."

Of course his father, Frank, lived to be 97. He farmed 160 acres and dug graves before his son—in a sense passing the shovel from father to son.

So you could point to heredity, except that his mother died at 36.

George is in a reminiscing mood at the mention of his father and mother.

The roots of few living persons in Chisago County go deeper than George Noren's. (His father spelled the name with one E but it can go both ways, George says.)

Frank Noren came to the area in 1869 from Sweden, pulling his boat on the St. Croix shore at Franconia. He made wooden Swedish shoes and harvested and then bought the farm. His wife, George's mother, was a Linn, whose family had come to the county in 1869, just a few years after the first three Swedes settled Minnesota near Hay Lake south of Scandia.

George and his first wife had eight children and there are descendants scattered all over the area.

As he speaks you notice, too, that George doesn't wheeze, doesn't pause to take a breath, never falters with a reply to a question.

He is a little hard of hearing but his hearing aid, properly tuned, solves that deficiency.

I prepare to leave that afternoon and his roommate, who had been kibitzing from behind the curtain room divider, sort of hobbled in to tell me that George is as agile as a boy of 20 and "look at me, I'm all crippled with arthritis. And I'm a lot younger than George, too."

"I'm only 93."

(February 13, 1980.)

Dallying in posh Wayzata

Wayzata. Will anybody who has spent a day browsing in Downtown Wayzata please raise a hand?

Neither had I until last week and it certainly is going to save me travelling afar to rub wallets with the folks of status in, say, Sausalito, Greenwich or Newport.

Wayzata, in Dakota Indian tongue means "WAZIAH"— the beneficent father of them all.

And he surely has been the Great Father for its residents, whose median income must be far beyond $20,000. The tourist or one-day visitor is invited to share this wealth and see how the other ten per cent live.

Curve off U.S. 12 toward Lake Street and the "Port of Wayzata" on Lake Minnetonka's Wayzata Boulevard sweeps across your vision. You sense that you are entering something as close to those utopian streets "paved in gold" as you will ever come.

The cars are more expensive, polished, finely-tuned; the women look chic as a *Vogue* ad; the men—even the few in jeans and jackets—are as fashionable as if they had posed for *Town & Country* magazine.

Even the teen-agers lope about in designer jeans, whirr by on shiny bicycles or in "personal" sporty, little cars, rustless and scratchless.

Streets are swept.

Lake Street is at its newly-remodeled best, tiny trees in low, bricked-trimmed flower and shrub beds; ornamental lamps.

Even the litter—and there is some, I regret to say—is posher than the ordinary bottles, cans and wrappers and paper bags. Only the best labels.

The visitor has four collections of shopping areas from which to pick—Wayzata Bay Mall, Wayzata Home Center, the Village and that curving wide ribbon—Lake Street. All are within walking distance and some are indoor malls, boasting 15 and 33 shops.

The people you meet on the streets and in the shops have come to buy linens, china, Dior originals, prestigious furniture, diamonds, antiques, old books at Whitely's cozy, Dickensian shop; stoves for fish houses and Georgian silver.

There are, perhaps, more "glitter" shops in Downtown Wayzata than any other community its size.

"And more people to buy the glitter," said a fellow browser.

Architecture is hip-mansard-roof, low, one story strips, squares, with an occasional thrusting two story building to break the skyline monotony, nearly all of it is new, synthetic. Very little of Downtown Wayzata will qualify during the next century for National Historic Site designation.

One picturesque, functional exception is the Wayzata Depot landmark of the late 19th century, set strategically between Lake Street, the Burlington Northern tracks and the Wayzata Bay port.

This has been retrieved from destruction and now houses the Wayzata Chamber of Commerce where I found the lady manager, an enthusiastic promoter of the "Wayzata Way of Life" and wearing an outfit that might well have come out of some "oval" room in a women's wear shop, any several of which I could see by peering out of the stationmaster's bay.

The depot, with its whitewashed brick, complements the gracious, easy charm of a town, which savors it as one would a comfortable heirloom sofa. It is the center, too, of James J. Hill Days each autumn, honoring the Empire Builder, who brought the railroad, the fashionable resort hotels and the wealthy guests to fill them.

Hill is gone, so are the resort hotels and passenger trains. But the affluent guests have become residents, settling into the mansions, villas and manors in the cul de sacs on the lakeshore.

"By the way," she said, "speaking of old-fashioned charm, you must mention the summer season of our own Lake Minnetonka packet boat, the "Lady of the Lake," which will run daily and on charters between the Excelsior and the Wayzata port, right in front of the depot.

"Sort of reverting to the days of James J. Hill, don't you know?"

She suggested that in my browsing I not miss Fred Betlach's jewelry-diamond-art shop, in a two-story, French-style building on Lake Street.

When you get hungry in Downtown Wayzata, there are three choices:

Chouette, reputed to be one of the best French restaurants in America, if not the most expensive. Lunch and dinner served here. And it might just be that for your first trip to Wayzata, you'd want to take that in. But don't expect to find it filled with a lot of the natives. They reserve Chouette for special occasions, too. Instead you'll likely find them across the street at Hart's Restaurant (since 1927), just remodeled and re-opened in spacious waterfront dining rooms, with an old "Wagon Wheel" motif and daily specials that are reasonable, home-cooked and tasty. The service and tradesmen eat at the counter in a front coffee shop, the others sit and linger long over lunches in the lakeside ambiance.

Or, you can hike down to the City Meats and have one of the lads make up a dazzling deli sandwich, with a salad on the side.

Then take this repast out and find a bench or a table or rock along the Boardwalk. From here you can sit and enjoy what its residents modestly call: "A Very Special Place." (April 4, 1980.)

Other Summit Avenue filled with history, too

Center City. Back in the 1880s builder Vilhelm "Willie" Carlson, not long from Sweden, used to take prospective clients up and down St. Paul's Summit Avenue in a horse-drawn wagon to look at houses.

"If you see anything you like," he told them, "I can build it for you out of wood."

Willie Carlson's houses, in a variety of styles, went up during the next 20 years along two curving blocks of Center City's own Summit Avenue, facing west across North Center Lake, "where the sunsets paint pictures."

With few exceptions, all 19 of them are his.

Preserved, restored and lived in by some descendants of original Swedish owners and new "pioneers" of gracious living, they now are on the National Register of Historic Places as a National Historic District.

Like their St. Paul Summit Avenue models, they are set back on broad, spacious lawns. Lot sizes are in the area of 90 feet wide and 200 deep.

Anchoring all of this as the district's *pièce de résistance* is Chisago Lake Lutheran Church at the north or Uppertown end of the avenue, which Carlson built in 1889 and which has long been on the National Register. It's not only a landmark but also the second Lutheran church congregation in Minnesota (May 1854) and citadel of the Augustana Synod.

"We think the Summit Avenue Historic District may be one of the most unusual, if not unique patches of Minnesota history," says Lloyd Hackl, professor of English at Lakewood Community College and one of the founders and first presidents of the Center City Historical Society.

He and his family "discovered" the street nine years ago and have restored to Victorian graciousness one of those Carlson homes, a Greek revival two-story house with an oriel jutting off the grand staircase.

But the real charms of the interior are the exquisite carving and decorating in woods done by Carlson, who used the solid oak wood that abounds in forests nearby.

The first owner of the present Hackl house was a distinguished county attorney, A. B. Slattengren. The residence was built in 1901, one of the last Carlson houses, on the high—or south—end of Summit Avenue.

Their home, with two massive Ionic columns framing the front entrance, is one of the show places along the avenue.

Behind Porter's is a small, yellow house that Carlson built for himself while he was building the other houses and where he lived until he put up his own mansion in 1905, says Hackl.

To stroll the two blocks, north to south, as Hackl and I did one afternoon, is like walking through time at the turn of the century.

He always likes to begin, not on Summit Avenue, but on old Main Street along Uppertown, connecting Summit at the church corner. On old Main is the Chisago County courthouse, built in 1876, still used as the oldest frame courthouse in Minnesota.

"You get the feel of Carlson's grand plans for Summit this way," Hackl says.

Just across the street from the church is the first Carlson home, a veritable mansion in Victorian style, with cupola gingerbread design painted yellow and white. It was built for F. G. Lorens, Center City implement and auto dealer. His grandson, Lorens Johnson, lives there now.

We passed a neat, red Gothic revival house and then the former homes of the Peterson brothers, Solomon and Elof, both prominent merchants.

Les Johnson, a retired architect and his wife, Lois, live in one of the most striking houses, one that has oval swirls and resembles an inverted ark with its curved front porch and pillars.

"A man named Goslin lived in the next house," says Hackl. "He went to Canada and brought back a bed that the King of England was supposed to have slept in. So everybody always called it the King's bedroom and him the King after that. He also created quite a stir by bringing home a Norwegian wife."

Tom and Karen Christiansen live in the Goslin home now and have just recently opened a malt shop in Lindstrom.

"I guess it was about 10 years ago that this awareness of history and the value of these homes really began around here," Hackl said.

"We began to realize what we had here. Mainly the Center City Historical Society developed from back-fence neighboring."

(December 4, 1985.)

Postmaster still paints

Wells. Whatever happened to Jack Horan, who lived at 1251 Portland Ave. in St. Paul, the kid who used to draw a lot at St. Luke's grade school?

His dad was William P. Horan, a lawyer and part of the city's Irish clan. He moved to Wells around 1937.

Well, Jack just made the big time with one of his paintings. Some artists wait a lifetime to show in New York City and others never get there. But there it was in the Ukrainian Institute on Fifth Avenue, signed "Horan."

In Wells, they call him the "Painting Postmaster." He's been postmaster for five years.

"Heck, he's got paintings hanging in half the offices and homes in Blue Earth County," one townsman said.

I drove down here out of curiosity.

The day I found Jack Horan in Wells was the hottest day of the year. The temperature had just broken 100 on the curb in front of the U.S. Post Office. The only time it's worse, they said, is during a blizzard.

There's a big mural on one wall of the post office. Jack painted that in 1971 when the postal service went "private." It shows the history of "carrying the mail" in America.

Jack has been painting seriously since 1964, but not prolifically.

"Getting all revved up to paint, studying, learning. Five years from now, when I may retire, then I'll begin to paint. What I'm doing now is what I can sandwich in between getting up at 4:30 a.m., starting to sort mail at 5:30 a.m. and working until 4:30 p.m. every afternoon. That's a long day. And with only one lung you can't spend a lot of time painting at night."

During the Korean War he lost 80 percent of one lung from tuberculosis and spent a year in Veteran's Hospital.

We went to Jack's house near the edge of town, a house he pretty much built across from a big grassy park on a yard that stretches back to a corn field, poised to spew forth rich, plump golden ears. Some of those ears were in a pot on Jack's kitchen stove.

"A fringe benefit of living in a country town," said Jack's wife, Marty, whom he met 25 years ago when she came into the post office to buy a stamp.

The house is filled with Jack's work and his collection of favorite artists' work—including prints of Dali and Picasso works.

"I've done perhaps 150 pieces since I began and most of it has either been given away, bartered for goods and services or sold."

What about the New York City art show?

"I studied with Lloyd Herfindahl, the widely known Albert Lea artist, and he is also a leader in the International St. Germain des Près Artists group, with headquarters in Paris. Anyway, they held their first International show in New York City back in June and Lloyd asked me to enter. It's the first thing I've ever had in any show and imagine opening in the art center of America."

Jack's painting wasn't, he says, his best style or effort. It was a painting—a sort of collage—of collectibles he has in his house: a big Mobil Oil gas pump sign, stained glass church window and a dollar bill.

"In fact, I was embarrassed that Lloyd picked that one, but I didn't have much around."

Jack needn't have worried. A German art dealer-buyer happened to browse the exhibit, was fascinated by Jack's painting and wants to see more. So he is expected in Wells any day.

Horan would prefer to show him work he likes better, his landscapes done in moody browns, blues, grays and greens that appealed to the Dutch painters, the British romanticists, the French Barbizon painters.

"My heroes are Millet, Ruisdael, Rembrandt and Gainsborough. Ruisdael and Rembrandt both painted Dutch landscapes of terrain much like that around Wells," Jack says.

"I go out four miles from my house and sit with a sketch pad on a spring or fall day when the land is rich with black soil mingling with browns and greens. The land reflects off the clouds, turning the whole into a blend of colors."

Jack sketches and paints "by the numbers."

"I block out each section on my sketch and write in the

colors I see, like I'll put down 'mud brown' or 'beer amber' and I remember in my head what it was like. So I get back to the studio and create that color on my palette."

Jack's studio is an old shed he converted into a cozy retreat about 15 yards behind his house. It is heated in winter and air-conditioned in summer, just about large enough for Jack, his easel and his shelves of art books. It is sans telephone because "in a small town the postmaster gets calls at all hours of the night."

"I call it my cocoon and my wife says I occasionally hatch a beautiful butterfly from it."

His best audience includes Marty and his two children, son Pat, a senior at Wells High School, and Theresa, a chemical engineering major at the University of Minnesota.

"We're used to Jack's almost Yoga-like immersion into art. He's a walking library of art history," Marty says. "They even call him from school with an art question."

Jack still considers himself a hopeful painter with no idea where he will go in style.
(August 1, 1980.)

Jail Guests "sentenced" to good bed, breakfast

Taylors Falls. The rumor was that a huge crime wave was happening in Taylors Falls because the old jail was filled almost every night.

The rumor was only half right.

There's no crime wave, but you can spend the night in the old Taylors Falls jail without even being arrested.

In fact, it's best that you reserve your place to sleep behind bars and check in with your "jailor" Helen White,

Chisago County historian, author and newspaper publisher. She owns the place and restored it two years ago into what is a unique bed-and-breakfast place.

The cozy, 16-by-24-foot, V-roofed wooden building at the foot of historic Angels Hill historic district stands shyly next to a more elegant Victorian building, where Helen lives, writes and publishes the annual *Dalles Visitor* magazine.

"It had been sitting there, and in 1981 I got the notion to do something interesting with it. And bed and breakfast seemed appropriate," she told me the other day when we sat rocking in what had been Cells No. 1 and 2, now a comfortable high-ceiling living room blending donated antiques and contemporary decor.

Cell No. 3, across what had been the cell block corridor, has become the dining-kitchen area, complete with cooking facilities and a tiny refrigerator stocked with "breakfast-makings"—eggs, fresh rolls, fruit juice, pancake mix and maple syrup. Coffee beans are available to be ground by an old fashioned hand grinder. Cell 4 is the completely contemporary, tiled bathroom with tub and shower.

Then there's the old attic, opened up into a spacious loft bedroom, reached by wrought-iron steps and railing, simulating a jail-like touch.

Two guests can sleep here and two more on couch beds in the living room. Then there's the second-floor door to a patio terrace and tiny English garden, hidden by a brick wall that prisoners used to scale with regularity.

The jail atmosphere has been carefully orchestrated by Helen to provide a little of the flavor, but with air-conditioning, comfort and none of the inconvenience.

Beautifully finished 2-by-four-foot dividers shaped like

cell bars separate the rooms and the old-fashioned but now shined pot-bellied wood stove still sits in the center of what once was the corridor.

"It's still used avidly by every guest who comes here in cold weather," Helen said. "Our biggest business comes in the coldest, snowy months when skiers and snowmobilers are here."

Then there's the original and slightly rusted outside iron door, last used for real in 1923, when the jail was closed.

"I wanted to buy the door, which was doing security duty at the municipal liquor store. I went through channels, but nothing happened because I found out the jail door had been stolen by the liquor store from the bank, which had stolen it from the jail. So I got it back to the jail for nothing."

Helen has tried to incorporate Taylors Falls-Upper St. Croix furnishings and add some worthy art. She had an original Adolf Dehn watercolor print, "August in Minnesota," on one wall. "I bought that in 1942, in New York City," she said.

A wood etching of Taylors Falls by valley artist Alexander Masley is on another wall and some watercolors by Helen's mother, 82 year-old Elizabeth McCann, hang in other spaces.

All of the eating ware is pottery created by three local artists—Janel Jacobson, Jeff Oestreich, and Linda Christianson.

Floor rugs are locally made.

The guest book provides entertaining reading.

Couples have honeymooned in the old jail. Police officers have deliberately come for a weekend as a novel way to vacation. A French couple wrote a glowing testimonial to

Helen in French, which Helen understands because she
spent a year in France. An Army officer in the Judge
Advocate General's office who heard about the jail wrote to
say he and his bride had two choices: The Fairmount Hotel
in San Francisco or the jail in Taylors Falls. They picked the
jail and were recommending it to everybody.

You can sentence yourself by writing Helen White, in
care of Historic Taylors Falls Jail, 102 Government Road,
Taylors Falls, Minn. 55084.
(September 16, 1983.)

Lutefisk beckons in Lindstrom

Lindstrom. It is that time of the year here when posters
announce Swedish lutefisk dinners in churches and a few
restaurants put lutefisk on their menus.

I usually find my way at least twice between November
and the first spring thaw to the Swedish Inn on Lindstrom's
Main Street for a dose of Myron "Pinky" Morrison's lutefisk
(Swedish spelling, ludefisk.)

In fact, I go to Pinky's place quite a few times during the
year even when lutefisk isn't on the menu because his
Swedish Inn is a rare exception to the great dearth of eater-
ies around the state paying tribute to Swedish cooking.

Not only does Pinky include Swedish items almost daily,
but his establishment is his version of a slice of old
Smaaland or Vasa in the Old Country. Even the location is
a natural.

Swedish Inn, with its patriotic Swedish blue-and-yellow
façade and flags, is almost across the street from the statue
of Karl Oskar and his wife, Kristina, fiction hero and hero-
ine of Vilhelm Moberg's trilogy, "The Immigrants," "Unto a

Good Land" and "Last Letter Home."

This proximity draws most of the hundreds of tourists and visitors from Sweden, who come each year to the land their ancestors settled. And after dutifuly paying tribute to Karl and Kristina, singing a chorus or two of the Swedish national anthem, they wipe away their tears and cross the street to try the food at the Swedish Inn.

On some days, Pinky and his staff come up with Swedish sausage or meatballs, tiny boiled potatoes with parsley and cream sauce herbed with allspice, Swedish style.

With it they might serve lefse or Swedish limpa bread. Then again, they might come up with platters of torsk and melted butter or cream sauce. "That is always on the menu, seven days a week, starting with breakfast," Heather, my waitress, told me the other day when I stopped in for lunch.

You could discover krumkake and herring salad, but lutefisk only comes on Fridays and Saturdays (maybe for Sunday brunch) during the holiday season and into the end of winter.

Or by popular demand.

Even Pinky's salad bar, well-known throughout Swede-land, from Chisago City through Lindstrom, Center City, Scandia and Copas, has a Swedish look and taste.

Those folks from Sweden always enjoy the plethora of Swedish artifacts, souvenirs and decorative touches. If he knows you're coming or you announce your Swedish backgrounds, Pinky or his waitresses will cover your table with blue paper tablecloths, use yellow paper napkins and set a big Swedish flag in the center. Sometimes, he dusts off some Swedish trolls or tomte, the good-luck fairy.

Huge pots of fresh, strong Swedish coffee come without asking.

But what excites the patrons, both Swedish and non-

Swedish, is the huge map of Sweden, posted on one wall. Visitors from Sweden are invited to fill out a card, writing whatever they choose, and tack it alongside the map, with a piece of yarn drawn to the area where they live in Sweden.

There are, perhaps, 100 of these cards, always changing, denoting visitors with a wide background of pursuits and interests and relatives living in Minnesota.

Members of the Swedish royal family have sent photos.

There still is enough Swedish spoken in the area to add that authentic touch to a meal eaten there. And on any one day, the front counter stools are filled with retired Swedish farmers and businessmen, drinking coffee, eating Swedish cinnamon toast, and talking Swedish.

Oddly, the creator of all this Swedish ambiance and cuisine isn't Swedish at all. But Pinky learned his Swedish cooking from cooks at nearby Hazelden Foundation, where he worked for a number of years.

Seven years ago, he left there and bought the Swedish Inn, and just in the nick of time for Swedish food fans. Because the only other cafes in town were sort of passing up Swedish style cooking. And you either got to the Lutheran church dinners or you didn't eat Swedish food.

The Swedish Inn staff members greet the lutefisk season with mixed emotions. They like to eat it—it is almost required eating—but they don't care about cooking it.

As Heather said, "One thing is for sure. You can tell whether it's being served the second you walk inside."

And for Lutefisk buffs like myself, you don't need a better welcome.

(November 4, 1983.)

Oliver's Travels

The book Oliver's Travels *was published in 1973. It contained a collection of columns about the first trips which my wife and I made to Europe. The best of these columns are reprinted here.*

He signed it Dali

Cadaqués, Spain. It is silly, I know, for me to look at my right hand back in the hotel and remember that only an hour ago it twice shook the already immortal hand of the artist Salvador Dali.

Or that my wife considers framing the Oliver Towne column, on which he wrote a message and signed the famed Dali signature.

But it all happened on the sun-splashed patio of Dali's terraced, white stucco home, topped by two huge eggs, overlooking the blue Mediterranean here in the picture book seacoast village of Cadaqués.

If our adventure proved anything, it is being at the right place at the right time and ignoring the warnings by almost every Dali expert we've read that this world's most eccentric, unpredictable artist never permits visitors in this, his escape from the turbulence of the Dali public across the mountains.

Frankly, we never imagined, deep down, that we would be any more successful. But, as we told the waiter at lunch, it would be fun to try.

He agreed, but belonged to the school of skeptics. Still he drew a small map of directions.

"The way is straight up the hillside, a long, winding street, with tall walls of gray flagstones . . . about a half mile . . . then you see the ruins of an old tower . . . an abandoned chapel with a cemetery around it . . . and then a narrow path goes down toward the bay and you will see the white eggs . . . That is it."

It was about 5 p.m. when we started out on foot.

Somewhere we had read that Dali's siesta lasts from lunch to 4 p.m.

Once we took a wrong turn, twice we were so tired we almost gave up; but a girl on a motor scooter routed us back on the right trail. Then we saw everything fall into place—the tower ruins, the chapel, the cemetery and—far below, at the bottom of terraces the two huge white plaster eggs rising above the multilevel, Spanish-modern house that Dali designed.

We walked slowly toward the shore. Suddenly we saw a man and woman come down a flight of steps and stroll slowly around the house toward another series of stairs.

"It's Dali," my wife gasped. "The mustache." And Gala—his long-time rudder, wife and companion.

She was right. We watched them. Dali carried a bunch of wild flowers in his hand. They glanced once at us and then climbed the stairs and we heard a door shut.

Opportunity lost?

We sat on a seawall, debating.

"There's only one way. Knock on the door and all he can do is shut it in our faces," I said.

Then good fortune. The caretaker came around the side of the house and kindly interceded for us with the white-uniformed housekeeper and cook.

"Go around and up the stairs to the front door. I will let you in," she said.

Seconds later we were actually inside the lower foyer of the house, with its Spanish-Dali decor in snow white, huge fireplace and a big stuffed grizzly bear, draped with Dali jewelry.

"Please, write your names and who you are and I will take the note to Dali," she said.

Three cheers for the housekeeper. She was cordial and optimistic.

We heard her footsteps returning. Would he or wouldn't he? My 51-year-old heart missed a beat.

Then she was back, smiling and beckoning us to follow her up several winding flights of stairs to the roof patio.

There he was, sitting in a wicker chair, in casual sports shirt, slacks and open-toed shoes, picking thistles off the wild flower stems.

The famous Gala, his inspiration for so many years, sat across from him.

"Bonjour," he said, half rising to shake our hands. We shook hands with Gala, too.

Dali is no longer the dashing figure he once was. He is in his 70s now and balding at the back of that famous head. But that face, with the curled mustache, is as familiar as wherever you see it.

There was no suggestion that this was the same man who leads his entourage to the Meurice Hotel in Paris, driving a monstrous Cadillac. Nor did he give a hint of the Dali who said, when asked if he took drugs, "Why should I? I am the drug."

He speaks good English, but prefers French.

There we stood, and what to say?

But it went smoothly.

For a few more minutes we talked about his art and its interest in St. Paul . . . his Dali plates being sold in stores . . . and how lucky it was we had found him here.

"We just got here for the summer from Paris," he said. Then we shook hands again. He waved to us. And we left, almost tiptoeing.

All the time we'd chatted, Dali and Gala had been busy stripping thistles for a bouquet of wild flowers they were making.

The walk back to the hotel was all down hill.

Eau de Cologne

Cologne, Germany. The traveler steps off the Cologne Express from Brussels. His eyes fill with the twin spires of the Cologne Cathedral reaching to the sky. His nostrils sniff the aroma of the second thing that has made this once Roman Empire city a household word in the world's boudoirs.

Eau de Cologne or just plain Cologne water.

It's an old story with a lingering fragrance and it begins here in the Cathedral shadows with a tiny bottle in a tiny room of a tiny museum, dedicated to making the world smell nice.

This tiny bottle on the dais bears the label of Johann Maria Farina, one of two Italians who came north to Cologne in 1709 with the recipe for a wonderful medicine called "L'Eau Admirable" (Admirable water).

For originally Cologne water was prescribed for all the illnesses then known to man.

It was even prescribed to be taken internally by the tea-spoonful. It is said that the alcoholic content, into which were dissolved the essences of flowers, would at least make one forget his sickness until the hangover next morning.

But that first Cologne water was listed as a pharmaceutical product until after the Napoleonic invasion, when it was decreed that the recipes of any magic medicines must be publicly disclosed.

This the Farina firm refused to do and had to change its grand scope of cures on the label to one which merely said: "for the care of the body."

It belonged to the soldiers of Napoleon, occupying Cologne, to provide the name by which the water is best known.

The Germans had called it merely: "Cologne or Kölnisch Wasser."

The French troops sent it back home to their wives and sweethearts and called it "Eau de Cologne."

And the world adopted that label.

And then it was shortened to "Cologne." Like so many other good things, imitations have literally flooded the earth. Almost any toilet water is called "Cologne," but like Coca-Cola, there is only one true Eau de Cologne and it is manufactured by 20 licensed firms here in the city that gave it the name.

The romance of Eau de Cologne is never-ending.

Long before Madison Avenue copy writers began to write with suggestive words about the alluring powers of Cologne, Wilhelm Raabe, the author, wrote in the 1700s—

"This drop of Eau de Cologne . . . contained Europe with all its culture and so relieved the fatal congestion in the blood and prevented a heart attack which threatened my life."

He must have drunk his drop.

The first Cologne was shipped to America in 1810. By that time, we were smelling pretty sour.

Belated as was its arrival on the dressing tables of American women, they made up for lost time.

Today American women—and lately men—are literally drenching themselves in the stuff, in worship of the fetish of smelling good.

Europeans, alas, from what I have sniffed on this trip, must be drinking theirs.

One of the most popular Eau de Colognes marketed is No. 4711, in a gold-leaf bottle.

Why something so pleasant should carry such a prosaic label has the aroma of a story.

Go back again to the occupation by Napoleon. The French troops, after a night on Cologne, had trouble finding their way back to their billets. So the commander ordered all buildings numbered.

One of these was a house No. 4711, owned by a man who made Eau de Cologne, but needed a distinctive name. He knew a good promotion gimmick and called his Cologne simply No. 4711.

And it has become one of the most sought after and bought after of them all.

But the label on that tiny bottle in the Eau de Cologne museum, bearing the name FARINA and the picture of roses, is still the oldest Cologne in existence, one of the first bottles ever produced.

And the same Eau de Cologne, with the same label, is sold today by the millions of bottles.

Only this is the true Eau de Cologne—it says here on the bottle.

Lunch at Julia Child's

Somewhere North of Nice, France. As Julia (The French Chef) Child and her husband, Paul, waved our car down the driveway from their "Escape Hatch" on a sunny slope filled with rose bushes in full bloom, my wife said, "when you write about it, skip the preliminaries. People will want to know what Julia served for lunch."

The setting for the first two courses was a shady patio and a table with an umbrella, the view looking across a secluded valley and the Alpes-Maritimes in the distance.

For an apéritif, Mrs. Child suggested Kir on the rocks (Vermouth and Cassis). We nibbled on cheese puffs.

(She drank an inverted martini—mostly vermouth and a little gin.)

Muralists from La Cité de la Création painted a series of murals called "Rue des Grands Chefs" on the walls of Paul Bocuse's restaurant in 1993. Shown here are James Beard and Julia Child filming her television program.

Next came what Julia called a "composed" salad—juicy, ripe tomato slices, lettuce, fresh green beans in vinaigrette sauce, stuffed eggs and tuna fish chunks with tiny Provence olives.

The tray was like a still life painting.

With it we drank white Pouilly Fuissé wine.

All the while we ate and got acquainted, a barbecue grill was cooking a leg of goatkin (young goat), a delicacy in this section of France.

But for this main course, with Paul carving, we adjourned to the dining room of the small, but functionally designed home of yellow stucco, with red tile roof and many over-hangs.

The goat was crusty on the outside with a mustard sauce coating and juicy and tender inside, tasting almost sweet and a little like lamb.

"There is no reason why American butchers shouldn't sell goatkin; it should be available," said Julia. "It's delicious."

And it was.

With the meat was served a ragout of Vegetable Provençal—fresh vegetables in a sauce made with fresh garlic. It didn't shout for attention, but everything folded into the other with a gentle, soft fragrance.

Paul decanted a bottle of Provence red wine for this course, over which we lingered in animated conversation.

Dessert was a sorbet of fresh strawberries, garnished with whole, giant strawberries dipped in fondant flavored with Kirsch. Beautifully done.

For coffee, we all walked a gravel path, lined with a rainbow of flowers, to the nearby home of Julia's mentor, friend and collaborator in *Mastering the Art of French Cooking,* Volumes I and II.—Mme. Simca Beck Fisch-bacher.

Simca—"you must call me that"— had broken a leg and sat at an outdoor patio table, the injured member in a cast, propped up on a cushion.

She served demitasse and immediately enveloped the scene with her vivacious effervescence. Simca is the model for the true French woman.

For a half hour, she cast her charm over us as she described her own book, *Simca's Cuisine*.

"The book goes beyond Volumes I and II and from north to south of France with Haut Cuisine. No basics. These are 250 recipes incorporating all the lessons Julia put into our first books. And there are my stories to go along."

Like the vignette about her grandfather, who put together the formula for Benedictine brandy.

"They always say, but was he a monk? He was a monk with 21 children," laughs Simca.

For the Childs, who built a home on land owned by Simca and her husband, their meeting in 1948 in Paris has been a warm and close human relationship.

They fit like fingers in a glove just as Paul and Julia have combined talents for food (she) and art, writing (he) in a marriage with enviable rapport.

At home in France, Julia is old-shoe, happy, and gracious and like that "wonderful cook and neighbor down the block."

The fact that she started a revolution in kitchen cookery is her great pride.

She beats the drums with her hearty voice about how housewives must unite and cook with fresh, live foods. And she sounds a scathing requiem for "all those dead foods that come in packages, fortified with all kinds of things."

Paul, whose painting blends realism with surrealism, is polished, the perfect host and a bit more reserved until, if you reach into a subject that delights him, he becomes a superb storyteller.

A retired U.S. government diplomat, who lived in Paris during the romantic 1920s and 30s, Paul is the steady hand on the throttle of the P & J express.

It was he who designed Julia's kitchen, which resembles a culinary laboratory. Paul was the architect of their home's interiors and his art has been widely exhibited.

He was painting the Sunday afternoon we were there—a new sign for their home.

"Only one request," he said. "If you write about being here, please don't give our location. Don't say where we are. This is our secret place."

I can say, though, that Bramafam-Pitchoune is a little bit of Heaven on earth for two very human beings.

I got hunter's stew

Paris, France. On the same day that Jordanians were killing Syrians and vice versa and world leaders were running around trying to snuff out lit fuses, my wife and I turned the corner near the Eiffel Tower and found that culinary temple of the ages—the Cordon Bleu cooking school. Temple indeed!

The trouble is that when you've read about the great Escoffier and his Cordon Bleu legacy, you expect to find it in a palace at the very least.

You could pass it walking fast. A modest blue sign at 24 rue du Champ de Mars, a small front door, flanked by show windows displaying cook books and utensils—that's it.

Just inside, in a tiny room, at 2:30 p.m. every day, bonafide students and visitors with invitations and 25 francs present themselves to Madame E. Brassart, who sits at a desk in severe black dress, cut one inch above the knee.

At Cordon Bleu, you do not walk up and say: "Hello, my name is . . ."

You present yourselves to Madame, who studies the engraved card, scrutinizes you, smiles and says: "Fifty francs for two, please. We will wait here for the door to the classroom to open."

So are maybe two dozen others, most of them young Americans, notebooks in hand, worried looks on faces.

This is the day of the final, oral examination for them and during the class we attended, they were summoned one by one into a basement torture chamber where Madame presumably gave them the third degree. They all looked shook when they returned to their seats.

The momentous moment at last. The door opens and you file into a classroom the size of a large closet. Along one end is a counter and behind it the kitchen, ovens, pots, pans, burners, sinks. But something is missing.

Not one electric cooking gadget like a can opener or blender or mixer.

"Zos theengs like meexers are awful for cooking . . . you weel make some theengs in them, but it will not be food," the master chef instructor, Monsieur Narses, told us later.

There is no air-conditioning and after the pots got hot and the ovens heated and everybody was breathing hard, it got stuffy, but there was nothing wrong with the smells.

Chef Narses is a TV producer's dream. He is huge, wears a high white chef's hat and tells droll stories—if you understand French—all the while he is working.

He has an apprentice helper, a thin, little fellow, who got a real workout doing KP.

"Today," he said in French, and everybody wrote that down. "We are going to create Oeufs Brouillés sur Canapés (scrambled eggs in toast cups) . . . Soles à la Dieppoise (poached sole baked in a béchamel sauce of mussels from Dieppe . . . and Oranges soufflés (oranges cut in half, hollowed, peaked and filled with orange-flavored filling of eggs, flour and whipped by hand until it stood up in the bowl)."

There was a time when I didn't think he was going to get it all done in two and a half-hours. Or ever. That was when he had laid out four big oranges, a loaf of Pullman bread of French descent; two big, very dead fresh sole from Dover; shallots, an onion, two pounds of butter, and a bowl of mussels in shells.

I suppose it's a little like the start of open-heart surgery. You get everything all opened up and laid out and then the audience tries to figure out where you go from there.

I'll say this. Chef Narses is also a magician.

I followed him most of the way through the orange soufflé, the mussels in their own broth and the care and cleaning of the sole.

But I lost the béchamel sauce somewhere on a back burner, plumb forgot about the rice pilaf to go with the sole.

According to my notes, what I ended up with was Hunter's Stew. The Cleveland banker sitting near me said his notes indicated that he would have come up with something which would have turned to concrete in 20 minutes.

But Chef Narses came up with Oeufs Brouillés sur Canapés, soles à la Dieppoise and Oranges soufflés.

And they were magnificent.

For Whom the Bell Tolled

Madrid, Spain. "He sat right here and . . . wrote parts of
For Whom the Bell Tolls!"

Gary and Janet Hiebert dine in Madrid, 1967.

I sat down at the table against the back wall of Antigua Casa Botín on Calle de Cuchilleros—and tried to imagine how it had been when Ernest Hemingway sat and ate at this table and wrote longhand on big sheets of paper, blotting up drops of gravy and wiping the juice from the crisp skin of a barbecued piglet from his chin.

Hemingway has gone. But not the Casa Botín and all the memories Don Antonio has of those years during the Spanish civil war and after World War II when "Papa" Hemingway made the place his office, home and social habitat.

The table is not marked and if I hadn't read a Hemingway story some months ago in which Casa Botín was a loving scene, I would never have gone there and asked Antonio if it were true and could I have the Hemingway table.

I must have struck a chord of nostalgia, if not hero worship, in Antonio. He not only ushered us to the Hemingway table, but spun worshipful tales about Papa—the dark, gloomy days of the Spanish civil war when Ernest was up front gathering facts for *For Whom the Bell Tolls* and hurrying back to Botín, then closed to the public, to sit and scribble his way to literary glory.

"He wrote at a table over there by the window in the afternoons and here at night," said Antonio. "But the last few years of his life he stopped coming here. People hounded him to death, I think. He no longer had privacy."

For Auld Lang Syne, Antonio served us Hemingway's favorite dinner—slices of Serrano ham, gazpacho soup, half of a Botín's original roast piglet, barbecued in special ceramic ovens and beyond doubt the most delicious pork I have ever eaten. It had the blend of bacon, ham, roast loin and delicate meat flavors I have never tasted before.

Then Antonio sent over a pitcher of the wine of the house and gave us the pitcher to take home.

As he once did for Papa Hemingway.

I almost suggested Antonio ought to mark the Hemingway table for tourists, but I decided Ernest would have abhorred the thought and Antonio, too.

Hemingway belongs to an age of Europe that is gone. Like F. Scott Fitzgerald and Gertrude Stein and all the others whose voices echo from the bistros of Blvd. St. Germain in Paris to the second floor of Casa Botín in Madrid.

My wife left Botín with a feeling of warmth for Antonio. When we made our reservation at his café and asked for Hemingway's table, Antonio sent confirmation to our hotel in the manner of a Spanish gallant.

He sent a huge bouquet of red carnations and iris to my wife, with this on the card:

"Welcome to Madrid! Your reservation is at 9:30!"

"Why don't you ever do things like that?" she said.

"I do other things," I said, "like taking you on trips to Europe so some guy can send you flowers!"

An editor once told me, on the eve of departure for a trip, not to write travelogues and reminiscences of museums and cathedrals.

But I must make an exception in Madrid. To come here and not mention the Prado museum is like going to Rome and not describing St. Peter's.

For the Prado is the home of 67 Peter Paul Rubens paintings, a vast exhibit of Goya's works, not to mention Velasquez, El Greco, Murillo, Ribera, Zurbaran, Van Dyck, Titian.

Such is the magic of this showplace of Madrid.

Bullfights and Flamenco dancers notwithstanding.

"But certainly you are going to see a bullfight in Madrid," said the porter at the Hotel, where we stayed.

"No," I said, "I have seen a bullfight in Plaza Mexico, the largest of them all. And at bullfights I always want the bull to win."

"You should not go to a bullfight in Madrid," he said with disgust.

Country festival

Kröv An Der Mosel, Germany. Just after noon that Saturday, we drove from Zell to Traben-Trarbach, where Peter and Gertrude Zerfahs waited lunch for us in their fine home on Mosel Boulevard.

Gertrude is the sister of St. Paul's Joseph Knoedgen, retired pioneer sausage-maker on Rice Street, and they had called at our castle and invited us to take part in the annual Weinkirmes (wine festival) in nearby Kröv.

So, at 4, after a feast on Mrs. Zerfahs' home-cooking— smoked and fresh pork, wine sauerkraut, sausage, mashed and boiled potatoes and salad from garden greens—we drove to Kröv and the village streets were hung with banners, the riverside park was turned into a county fair of bratwurst and wine stands and in the center, from the statue of the Kröv wine king, flowed a half dozen streams of wine, which were sold by the glass to crowds clogging the square. Busloads of tourists and Mosel Madchens (Mosel maidens) strolled in bunches.

But our destination was the house and winery of Herr Wilhelm Muellers, whose family has produced vintages for generations. There we gathered him, his wife, and two sons and went off to the famous Kröv wine prober (wine tasting) in the Festival Hall.

Places for 300 were set, with a small glass in front of each, a tray of hard rolls and an empty bowl.

Now, at 5, began the two-hour tasting of 25 wines, from the ordinary to the great Spaetleses and Ausleses which sell for up to $30 in St. Paul when you find them.

While the Mosel Wine queen presided, dirndl-dressed daughters of wine-makers and uniformed sons of wine-makers paraded out from the backroom with bottle after bottle of wine.

Those with a sense of propriety sipped each wine, then poured the rest into a bowl, broke off a piece of roll to clear the palate for the next wine.

It was an amazingly serious group at first. Quiet and subdued. But some did more than sip. They kept finishing their little glasses instead of pouring the rest into the bowl as those in our party did.

And, as the evening wore on, voices rose, laughter filled the hall, the speeches got longer and more poetic and an air of festivity and conviviality reigned. For the select "wine probers," who had wangled invitations, this was an annual opportunity not to be missed.

Down in the winding streets and square, thousands more—all of whom owe their livelihood directly or indirectly to winemaking—were frolicking with more zest and uninhibited pleasure. The Mosel maidens paired off with single boys, the little wine cellar entrances poured sounds of music and hilarity out into the chill, drizzly night.

There was the moment in the Festival Hall when the 25th wine, a 1969 Kröver Letterlay Feine Auslese was announced and the man next to me smiled proudly.

His name was Schnitzius and it was one of his wines that ended the "Prob" with distinction.

Having survived the tasting of 25 wines, only parachuting from a plane is left as a challenge.

Herr Muellers led us once more through the streets, now boisterous with the high hilarity people made on their progressive wine drinking rounds.

It would, he said, last until 4 a.m. and begin all over Sunday and end Monday, appropriately, with a coffee and cake party in all the cafés and homes.

Something over 10,000 litres of wine are consumed during these three-day tributes to Bacchus, but Herr Muellers said that as yet, Kröv has never been drunk dry.

We adjourned to his home, where Mrs. Muellers produced plates of open-faced sausage and cheese sandwiches, coffee and cookies. Two French journalists from Paris had joined our entourage and we sat chattering in conversations that mixed perfect German with fractured French and English.

But everybody seemed to "compris" and "verstehe" and understand.

I will now recite the legend of the famous Kröv Nacktarsch (bare bottom) wine, as Herr Muellers told it.

Long ago, in fact very long ago, two little boys wandered down into a wine cellar in Kröv and began to sample from the various barrels.

They were discovered by the wine-maker, who yanked down their trousers and proceeded to tan their bare bottoms.

Henceforth the picturesque Kröv Nacktarsch name and label, depicting the scene—except that for export to the puritanical United States, the bare bottoms are covered.

Picnic, château style!

St. Emilion, France. It had been one of those glorious early autumn mornings, cloudless, lazily warm and calm. And we had spent it with Monsieur Alain Querre, touring the grape vineyards of Château Monbousquet, which he and his father own.

His English-born wife, Sheila, had driven up the poplar-shaded driveway with a Dutch free lance photographer and his tall, statuesque wife in a sheer, one-piece pantssuit. We were sitting in the elegant dining room of the 18th century, limestone château of Renaissance style. It is the way I have always seen a château in my mind.

"And now," said M. Querre, "we will have a picnic lunch in the garden. Come, let us enjoy the outdoors."

On the way to the picnic table, covered with red-flowered cloth, we passed two maids, setting a fire in a pile of grape branches.

"We will grill the meat over grape branches," said M. Querre. "Or rather the girls will . . . please sit down."

First came a huge platter of sliced, fresh, red tomatoes, in oil and vinegar, which we ate and then mopped up the dressing with big chunks of golden-crusted French bread, baked that morning in château ovens.

M. Querre served us one of his best red wines, a Château Monbousquet 1964 (about $10 a bottle) from a large pitcher.

Out beyond the garden, fringed by yellow African flowers the shape of mums, the lawns spread toward a duck pond, arched by tiny footbridges. Beyond, in the sun, lay the grapevines, heavy with purple bunches.

We talked, in both English and French, about ourselves, our lives, the travels we had made. But not once was there concern over the rest of the world's crises, wars, tensions, politics. Only the placid talk of new friends and gracious host and hostess.

Then the two little maids came hurrying up with huge platters of grilled steaks, an inch and a half-thick, and surrounded by almost yellow French fried potatoes.

M. Querre passed more French bread and we ate a picnic—château style.

There were seconds of both steaks and potatoes and then a soft lettuce salad—the tomatoes had been an appetizer—with fresh tarragon ground into the dressing.

M. Querre excused himself and returned with another pitcher of wine.

"You have tried my 1964. Now I will let you sample a younger 1968, not as full-bodied yet, but young and interesting ... You are the writer ... You find the words or don't find any, but simply say you enjoy it ... as you would a painting."

There were a half dozen kinds of cheese with this nectar, more bread and finally coffee, strong from newly ground beans.

The sun had passed its zenith by now. It was nearly 3 p.m. The shadows from the big oaks and lime trees began to lengthen across the château's park, ringed by a gravel road.

Each of us had told of experiences, of philosophies and little anecdotes about our countries, the Dutch photographer about his work for magazines, especially cookbooks, which use illustrations.

Our host taught a layman's lesson in the story of wines and the living they earn for the people of the Bordelais country, the blends of grapes used, the ways in which the wine growers police themselves to insure that Bordeaux wines are honest representations of the label.

M. Querre spoke, too, of a trip to the California vineyards he made and had high praise for the American wines.

He quoted us a letter, just arrived, from an English couple, who had read an exaggerated account of how St. Emilion château owners had taken up breeding thoroughbred horses.

"They are coming to see our horses . . . and we have none in the whole valley . . . except Pompidou—the name of our donkey out there in the field. We will have to fill them full of wine and then show them Pompidou."

The enchantment of the afternoon was broken by the beep of an auto horn—the first noise we had heard. Two ladies had come to fetch us for further touring. The Dutchman and his wife had to be on their way.

"What has amazed me," I said in parting, "is that we have spent part of an afternoon with no worrying talk, no bemoaning the fate of the world."

In reply, M. Querre handed me a spearhead-shaped stone.

"When we are too much with the modern day world," he said, "we just go out in the field and dig up these relics of men who lived here 20,000 years ago. Then it all comes into perspective."

Where "Silent Night" was born

Oberndorf, Austria. The road bends and twists down the long Alpine foothill in the Austrian Tyrol. Fresh, wet snow from a storm clung to the regal pines. The air was fresh, cold and flavored with wood smoke.

"What a wonderful place to write a Christmas carol," said my wife. "I know how he must have felt that night."

The little Volkswagen nosed into the valley at last and it was getting quite late in the afternoon, but we had a rendezvous with a song.

Woodcutters wearing Tyrolean hats and black boots stood and waved from the roadside. The town lay in the valley. The sign said: "Oberndorf."

An old woman, wearing a black shawl on her head and carrying loaves of bread, pointed the way.

A small, modest marker took up where she left off and we curved into a back street.

There it was. No longer a church, but a chapel, tiny and circular, remnants of the great church of St. Nicholas as it was before the flood of 1900.

Dirt was plowed around it, preparation for some further landscaping of this world shrine.

We parked the car and walked up the muddy alley toward the small, miniature Baroque-style building with the cross. Would the door be open?

It was.

The chapel was cold, damp and empty. On the outside door were carvings of two angels and this inscription in Austrian:

"Peace on Earth, Good Will Toward Men!"

Inside on the right was a wooden stand with a guest book and ballpoint pen.

Two stained glass windows told the story.

I looked at one, a portrait of a man, busily writing. Under it were the notes of the song. And I began to hum even before I read the words:

"Portrait of Franz Gruber! On this site at Christmas in 1818, he wrote the music of Silent Night, Holy Night! And here it was heard for the first time on Christmas day."

I looked at the stained glass window opposite.

It was the portrait of a priest, hand cupped to one ear to listen. Under it the inscription:

"Joseph Mohr, humble priest who wrote the words to Silent Night, Holy Night."

Had Father Mohr been on that pine-lined mountain road we had just taken into the village? Had he walked there on that bitter, cold Christmas eve of 1818?

He had gone to a small hut to baptize a baby. On the way back to the village, his heart was heavy. Bad times had befallen the community. The winter was terribly cold.

And mice had eaten holes in the church organ bellows. There was neither time nor money to make repairs and what music would there be for Christmas morning?

He was walking through the silent town when he met Franz Gruber, the schoolmaster.

Then, Father Mohr remembered that Franz had a guitar and sometimes wrote songs.

The priest asked if Franz would help and the schoolmaster eagerly agreed.

As the story is told, the two men hurried through the village to the church. And as they did, both were suddenly aware of the stars in the sky, hanging so low that one could almost reach up and touch them.

All night the two men worked, Franz writing the music and Father Mohr the words. It was a simple song, they agreed. But it could be played on a guitar.

Christmas morning, haggard, weary, the priest and schoolmaster had finished their song in time for services.

Then, while Father Mohr celebrated mass at the altar, he heard Franz Gruber's guitar playing the song for the first time in public.

At first the worshippers just listened. Then, with hastily written sheets of words, they began to sing—and their voices carried out of the little church, across the village. The music echoed against the Tyrolean hills and mountains.

But the people of Oberndorf guarded their song from crossing the Alps until they had gathered enough money to repair the organ bellows.

Then the schoolmaster tried the song again on the organ and an organist in the church who heard began playing it from village to village in the mountains.

At last four musicians from Oberndorf played and sang it at the Leipzig Fair of 1831 and the world passed it along to the ages.

Strangely the men who wrote it died poor and unrecognized in their lifetimes. Even now, the chapel, reconstructed at the site from ruins of the old church, is barely marked and little publicized.

As I stood in the chill of the April dusk recalling the story as they tell it in the village, I remembered all the times I have heard "Silent Night" sung and played at Christmastimes.

As a small boy at my grandmother's house around a Christmas tree. By carolers on city street corners. In a French boxcar on Christmas eve of 1944 during World War II. And in the great St. Paul Cathedral by the Cathedral boys' choir.

Now, when Christmas comes again, I will always remember the twilight of a day in the chapel at Oberndorf.

My wife added our names on the guest book to those thousands of others who have been in the place where the song "Silent Night" was born!

Innocents abroad

Segovia, Spain. If the typing seems a little shaky, don't blame the machine.

I've just done another stint with a car on Spanish highways.

And I may write a sequel to Hemingway's *Death in the Afternoon* called *Motoring in the Afternoon!*

It's just as deadly as bullfighting.

The two worst places to drive a car in Spain are Madrid and Toledo. (Also Barcelona.)

I learned in Madrid and graduated in Toledo. For a post-graduate degree, I drove 200 miles through the Gredos Mountains and have just found my way to the Grand hotel in Segovia.

If you can find your way to the Grand in Segovia, you can find your way anyplace in the rest of the world blindfolded. The first thing to remember about driving in Spain is put gasoline in the car.

Our little, stripped down SEAT was delivered to our Madrid hotel promptly and the man from the auto agency turned it over to us as a father would turn his son over to the wicked world—reluctantly.

He left, with backward glances. We got in and started the engine. "Oh, look," I said, "that red light blinks on the gas gauge. A novel touch."

Just then the hotel porter ran out and shouted:

"The man who brought the car happened to tell me there isn't much gas in it. Only enough to go six kilometers. About three miles."

And the nearest gas station—2.5 miles.

"With a tail wind, good directions and the Lord's help we may make it," I said.

In Spain you always make the sign of the cross before pulling away from the curb. Even if you're not Catholic. On this occasion I asked my wife to join me.

It is one thing to begin your European driving in Madrid on Sunday afternoon. But to begin—and realize you are almost out of gasoline—is quite another gray-haired crisis.

The rule in Spain is to be calm and blow your car horn. You blow the horn at pedestrians, to gain the right of way, to pass, to stop, to alert pretty girls, to enter intersections and leave.

When a thousand cars, streaking for the same plaza circle, where there is no speed limit, all blow their horns and you are looking for the right street to the gasoline station—brother, you are in a situation where the alarm better ring so you can wake up and find out it was only a nightmare.

We didn't find the right street to the gas station. We got lost. In the heart of Madrid.

I was trying to figure out the traffic signals, find the turn indicators, and honk the horn. My wife was trying to direct me from the map in her lap. And the red light kept blinking on the gas gauge, warning me it would soon be over.

I had more than visions of running out of gas in the middle of a four-lane street in Madrid.

We went right, then left. The trouble was that the porter at the hotel, in drawing a line to the gas station with a pencil had obliterated the name of the street on the map.

We didn't know where-in-Madrid we were!

The last resort was to pull up and ask a pedestrian.

"Gasolina?" I inquired.

He broke into a flood of Spanish. My wife wrung enough drops of comprehension out of it to determine that if we followed certain shadows from the sun, the gasolina was about six blocks away.

Then I almost drove past it. With a screech of brakes, I U-turned and came into the station from the wrong direction. Against the grain of traffic. It wasn't the last time.

Once the tank was filled with gasolina, merely focusing attention on the traffic situation was a lark.

Until we reached Toledo.

Toledo is known to the ages as the citadel of the artist El Greco, whose home and works are preserved as if he were the George Washington of Spain.

Toledo also is the most perfect driver's training and proving ground in the world. If you can drive in the walled city of Toledo, you can drive anywhere, anytime, in complete safety.

Unfortunately, by then men in white jackets will have taken away your car keys and hauled you off to the Funny Farm.

Toledo is compressed on a hill, completely walled. It was laid out in circles, which gradually get smaller until they converge in the main square of town.

El Greco's son was the architect for "modern" Toledo and he must have been drunk. Or a man of no vision. All the streets, laid out in the 15th century, are one quarter the width of an American city street without sidewalks. Houses and buildings abut the streets, except for two-foot passageways for pedestrians. So it is very dramatic when pedestrians and traffic try to negotiate the same street at the same time.

Two-way traffic is, of course, impossible. Every street in Toledo is one-way and you have to follow the circles, clockwise, to get where you are going.

Of course some mad engineer decided to connect the lines of the circle with little streets going here and there, crossing from one circle to the next.

And since there are no signs of direction, except some vague arrows, who knows where to go?

I thought I did. I drove the wrong-way on almost every street in Toledo. I bruised my horn finger from pushing down on the button.

I will never forget the image of those pedestrians, flattening themselves against the building walls, as my car met another, head on.

The other motorist stopped, waved and smiled and backed up. I waved and smiled and backed up.

"I think we took the wrong turn somewhere," said my wife. "We want to go to the Cathedral."

I could see the Cathedral all afternoon, but I couldn't seem to get there by car. I knew the Village Square was where the map said it was, but I never got there either.

Then I remembered an old rule of the thumb in football: When in doubt, punt!

I parked the car in a widening of the street.

"Come on," I said. "We'll walk."

A man in uniform came over and handed me a ticket.

"Your parking permit," he said. "You can park in Toledo all day for 20 cents—anywhere."

"By the way," I said, "Where am I?"

"At the Cathedral," he said.

I got out of town somehow. I guess the word had got out that a stranger was in town. We had virtually a police escort pointing the way at every turn of indecision.

I got back to our hotel on the mountain outside the walls—a former monastery—and took a hot bath and made the sign of the cross. That night, after dinner in a rural restaurant, my wife said:

"Just one more thing. Let's take a drive through Toledo at night. I've always wanted to see it in the dark."

I already had!

The open road in Spain is pleasant if you stay mainly on the plain, but my wife had Segovia on the itinerary for our last night on the road, which involved crossing the Gredos mountains at 6,700 feet on a narrow, winding road the Romans built and not one stone has been changed.

The last five miles into Segovia are on a road that would make a plowed field seem like a freeway.

It was late afternoon.

"This time," said my wife, "I don't have directions to the hotel." We stopped a policeman, directing traffic under a viaduct the Romans built. (I may try that out of town.)

"You can't miss the Grand hotel," he said in Spanish which my wife understands.

But we missed it.

We found other interesting places. A hospital, a monastery where the brothers were somewhat surprised to see a car—with a woman in it—pull through the cloistered gates.

We found the post office, the tourist bureau and a Spanish bookie named Sam.

The Grand hotel is the best hotel in Segovia. And certainly it ought to be reachable. Others must have.

Well, we finally drove down a one-way hill the wrong way, turned onto a street and there was the Grand hotel.

Out rushed a porter.

"I am so sorry, he said. 'You have just driven down a pedestrian mall. We park our cars a block up on the hill in the Cathedral lot. And we walk down a block to the hotel."

So I was vindicated.

You can't drive to the Grand hotel in Segovia.

But I did!

Toujours France!

We made our first trip to France in 1964 and returned twenty-eight times, so that we figured we spent about four months there. Paris was our favorite destination, but we roamed France from one end to the other—Provence, Brittany, the Mediterranean coast, Normandy, the island of Belle Isle, the cities and towns and hills—Marseille, Nice, St. Tropez, Lyon, Beaune, Avignon, St. Paul de Vence, and Bordeaux.

We dined at some of the legendary restaurants, feasted al fresco along many a roadside, rode the swift TGV trains, found Van Gogh's grave and made several visits to Monet's gardens, did the Louvre and celebrated the 100th anniversary of the Eiffel Tower.

We heard great operas in the Paris Opera House and followed in the footsteps of Gertrude Stein, F. Scott Fitzgerald and Ernest Hemingway.

The columns that follow tell stories of those wonderful years in France.

Picture-perfect scenery discovered in French village

Auvers-sur-Oise, France. It was late afternoon when we trudged up the long hill to the plateau and the cemetery where Vincent Van Gogh is buried.

Just behind us was the church he made famous by painting a picture that hangs in the Louvre's Jeu de Paume gallery and is in all the picture books of art. "L'Église de Vincent Van Gogh" (Vincent Van Gogh's church), it says.

Apparently Van Gogh took artistic liberty and painted out the trees that obstruct the view, or the horse chestnuts were planted later. The church is impossible to photograph from the same vantage today.

A layer of clouds covered the sun as we walked past the wheat fields he also painted into history. The cemetery is just beyond and ringed by four depressing gray stone walls with two wrought iron gates.

There is no arrow pointing the way once you are inside. But the photos in all the books show the grave to be set against one wall. We found it on the first try.

The marker is simple: "Ici repose Vincent Van Gogh" (Here lies Vincent Van Gogh) and the dates of his birth and death—in 1890—which came after a self-inflicted gunshot wound, although there is some mystery about that.

Next to Van Gogh lies his brother, Theodore, who died a year later. He was the one person who believed in the painter's work before anyone else.

A bed of flowers and green, leafy foliage blankets the two graves.

That's all there is to see.

They have been there for more than 90 years.

My wife and I stood there in the solitary silence and suddenly both of us felt a little chill. A few drops of rain fell.

As we started back down the hill into the village, two boys on mopeds blasted past us and broke the spell.

That night on the Rue Charles de Gaulle, the main winding street, we ate in a restaurant next to Maison de Van

Gogh, the café-restaurant-bar above which was his room and where he died. You can see it on certain days of the week. We were there on the wrong days and could not find the person with the key.

Up one street and a few blocks away is the residence of Dr. Gachet, whom Van Gogh painted in another popular painting. There is also a painting of the doctor's daughter and the story persists in the village that the doctor thought the artist was falling in love with his daughter and sped Van Gogh's death.

If Van Gogh haunts the picturesque, placid village sprawling along the banks of the Oise, so do a coterie of other painters: Camille Corot, Jules Dupre, Honoré Daumier, Camille Pissarro, M. de Vlaminck, Paul Cezanne and Paul Gauguin.   They all came here and painted because of the light and scenery, each in his time.

Just down the hill from the Van Gogh church is a tiny triangular park on which is situated a large statue of the artist Daubigny, standing with his palette and brush in hand.

At the tourist office two ebullient, efficient women spell each other on duty to assist the tourists who find Auvers. Mme. Dupont had corresponded with us, but Mme. Barolo was on duty and waiting with a sheaf full of booklets, pamphlets and materials on the Auvers Art Colony of the 19th century.

"We are called the Village of Painters," she said, suggesting that while Van Gogh may have become folk hero of the village, the others were no slouches.

"Almost every place in this village where you walk and in the nearby villages are represented in priceless, noted paintings done by one of these painters," she said.

"It is, next to Paris and Barbizon, probably the most painted place in France."

I thought about that two days later when, in the Jeu de Paume in Paris, I stood viewing some of those paintings and heard other tourists and visitors exclaiming over them.

They ought to go and see where it was done.

(October 14, 1981.)

Famous artists and writers good company in Barbizon

Barbizon, France. We walked through the garden of trees and tables from our room in Les Charmettes Hotel and passed through the iron gate onto La Grande Rue. Immediately we began walking with the famous artists of the Romantic French period called the Barbizon school.

Millet, Daumier, Courbet, Corot, Rousseau and Diaz were the stars. But there were a score of lesser masters who made this tiny, bucolic village famous in the mid 19th century—like J. K. Bodmer who also painted from nature and Indian scenes in the Minnesota area. Also joining us for a stroll on that fresh, sunny September morning were Robert Louis Stevenson and George Sand, who found the land and the forest perfect for their writing, just as the artists did for their canvases.

It is best to begin at the western edge of La Grande Rue, where the village abruptly meets the vast, dim, tranquil beauty of the Forest of Fontainebleau. We started down the street, just as Jean François Millet, artist Charles Jacque and their families walked out of the same woods down the same cobbles in June 1849 in a rainstorm, bedraggled but hopeful.

Our route took us past the Hôtellerie du Bas Bréau, where Stevenson stayed while he wrote his "Forest Notes."

It is a rustic, plush hotel and restaurant now and poor Stevenson probably could not afford to pay today's $80 to $90 a night for lodging, or the $40 to $50 price of dinner.

We come, at last, to the heart of it all, the Museum Auberge Père Ganne, in the center of "downtown" Barbizon, once the most famous inn south of Paris. Père Ganne was a part-time tailor; his wife kept the local grocery store. In 1824, the first contingent of artists arrived to commune with nature. The Gannes turned their two-story, sprawling building into an inn, the first for Barbizon.

By the mid-1860s, when Millet, Jacques, Corot, Daumier and Rousseau arrived, the place was a thriving hotel-restaurant-bar-grocery store.

There were few private suites at the top of the wooden staircase. Big rooms filled with cots were more in vogue. Downstairs was the crude foyer and lounge, an austere place of hard chairs and a fireplace that smoked as it heated the place in the dead of winter. To pay their way, many painters who later became world-renowned brushed scenes on the walls, woodwork and wardrobes.

There was a wine room and bar, the center of the robust drinking and boisterous laughter of the artists. All around in the corners were easels and artists' paraphernalia.

Innkeeper Ganne was shrewd. Every artist-in-residence had to turn over all his money before he could sign the register. These sums and whatever commissions came from sales were used to pay for food, drink, clothes and accommodations.

In the 1980s, a group of 55 Barbizon artists who still live and paint here have tried to recreate some of that ambiance in a next-door bistro-bar. But their enthusiasm is not matched by their talents in most cases.

The phantoms in our wake accompanied us to the edge of Barbizon's southern fields where, just to our left, are the lands where Millet found his gleaners and the pious couple for his immortal paintings.

We walked over their stubble. The harvest had come and gone. Machines had baled the hay, and the grain had gone to market. The gleaners had left, along with the romantics who painted them.

During our walk after dinner, we found the village locked up for the night, the windows shuttered by wooden slats, light filtering around the edges. There are muffled sounds of camaraderie but we had to hurry back through the silent, darkened village, so close and yet so far from the fizz of Paris.

The ghosts of the Barbizon painters bid us goodnight as the wrought iron gate to our hotel, where "madame" was waiting for the stragglers before closing us in for the night, safe and cozy from the outside world.

(October 9, 1981.)

French history comes alive
on the street where he lives

Paris. We had been staying in L'hotel Angleterre at No. 44 Rue Jacob on the Left Bank for three visits before we realized that the street itself was filled with ancient and modern French history, which touched the world and still does.

Jacob Street, all two blocks of it, is so deceptively modest with its narrow cobbled paving, narrower sidewalks, and buildings with routine façades that the average pedestrian is cheated out of its past unless he or she reads certain books on Parisian history.

It is not enough to know, as we did earlier, that our little hotel with the garden courtyard was once the British Embassy, hence the name change from L'hotel Jacob in the late 1920s; nor that when they arrived during a cold, wet Christmas season of 1921, Ernest Hemingway and his first wife, Hadley, settled in at the Jacob, recommended by another American writer, Sherwood Anderson.

The Hemingways found it "clean but very simple," and Hadley recalled the holes in the stairway carpets which Ernest referred to as "traps for drunken guests." New carpets have just been installed.

When one strolls along this short, shy little street, brushing against fellow walkers, jumping out of the way of the occasional auto, one should also know that Hemingway and his friends ate at the Pré aux Clercs, which still stands at the corner of Jacob and Rue Bonaparte and still serves simple but presentable meals.

Just across Bonaparte is the Hotel d'Isly, which is one of the other cozy, comfortable hotels on the street. About a century ago, composer Richard Wagner lived there and was so enchanted by the place that he wrote parts of "Tannhauser" in his spare time.

Down the street at No. 20 is another picturesque swatch out of Rue Jacob's past, which we can just peer in or through as we pass.

This was the salon of New York's Natalie Barney, novelist, short-story writer, poet, reporter, columnist and painter, about whom swirled the Women's Lib movement of the 1920s through 1960s.

Her Friday afternoon soirées, which included many famous personalities, were the origin of the word "bash."

"We would have 20-60-100 people. We served sandwiches, cakes, fruits, crystallized strawberries, tea, port, gin, whiskey," wrote Madame Berthe, her cook. The Michel Debrés, he a confidante of Charles De Gaulle and Pompidou, now own the Doric-columned temple, masked to the outside world. Two gendarmes stand guard day and night, which explained to us their presence. We had always thought the place was being raided.

You have almost reached the end of tiny Rue Jacob at Rue de Seine, the threshold of the boisterous Latin Quarter.

Nowadays, the street still tries to keep up with its vivid past. Every day when we walk out of our hotel and turn left to Bonaparte, we pass the tapestry and Oriental rug salon of a vivacious, loquacious German baroness, Sylve, who is a friend of Albert Lea artist Lloyd Herfindahl.

The ground-floor shops harbor some of the most exclusive Paris art galleries and dealers, places where the works of select artists are shown to prospective buyers from around the world—most of them with Arabic names just now.

There are four or five friendly, worthy little cafés, bistros and restaurants on the street, too. One of them is at No. 22, the Rotisserie de l'Abbaye, a medieval nightclub that recreates the history of the entire St. Germain des Prés area, along with food of the time.

One we found on this trip, just across the street from our hotel, is called simply 35 Rue Jacob. It seats barely 30 people in its quiet, candlelit dining room, a warm, homey, cozy refuge for us on a rainy night in Paris.

All this, on Rue Jacob, the street where we live in Paris. (October 6, 1981.)

Expatriates of the '80s

Carcassonne, France. The two young men playing guitars were performing in the plaza at sundown in the walled city of Carcassonne in southern France. They sang French ballads, American songs of the late 1960s and early 1970s. They were good.

Coins rained into the wide container one of them passed around to us sitting at the tables, sipping our coffee, pastis, and Perrier with lemon.

I said to one of the singers: "You speak English like an American."

"I was," he replied. "Born in New Jersey, but I've lived in France most of my life. My partner is a Belgian."

Later that night, down the street in a restaurant, a trio of musicians—young people from Spain—played music roaming from café to café.

In the little square intersecting Rue de Seine and Rue Jacob in the Paris Latin Quarter, you see them sleeping in empty packing cases behind a cement bench, sipping their bottles of cheap French wine, munching on thick sandwiches, playing harmonicas or violins. Begging.

They are part of a shuffling, bedraggled army of young people in their 20s, roaming Europe—some for the summer, some for the winter and some for as long as they can remember.

They dress in tattered jeans, wear floppy hats, beards. The women are casually dressed, always in granny dresses or jeans.

They are from everywhere, a polyglot of nations. You see them with backpacks, trudging along the platforms in the Metro stops.

One afternoon at the Boulevard St. Germain des Prés Metro stop, we listened as a young man playing a flute drew a large crowd with his renditions of Mozart, Beethoven and Chopin. He placed a cap nearby for donations. He was still there five hours later when we came back.

The cavernous corridors of the Metro stops echo to music—from country and western to the dance wave called reggae.

The huge plaza in front of Pompidou center—Paris fine arts focus in Beaubourg—is like a six ring circus all day and into the evening as troops of this odd army entertain by singing, playing, eating fire, swallowing swords, putting on skits.

In some corners, like that in front of Café des Deux Magots, the elite of these gypsy entertainers draw crowds so large that gendarmes wait in vans, hidden furtively around the corner, in case anything erupts into a brawl or melee.

We saw these young people sitting on the sidewalk, leaning against the American Express building, that American island in Paris. Inside, they could get ice water to drink and use clean restrooms, but obeyed the signs which say: "No backpackers permitted to loiter. No sleeping."

These are the young people who make pilgrimages to the grave of their hero, rock singer Jim Morrison, in Père Lachaise cemetery and sit in contemplative adoration, sipping wine and pouring the dregs on his plot and scrawling obscenities on the tombstones around his grave.

Late at night, as we walked back to our hotels in any place we stayed, we saw them: tired, weary young men and women, with haunted looks and bending from the weight of their earthly belongings on their backs.

In towns with youth hostels, they find warmth, food and companionship for a few dollars a night. But in Paris, they inquire at the desks of the little hotels and usually they are greeted with signs saying: Complet (full).

Somehow they get their act together long enough to collect a few francs for a hard roll, piece of cheese, a can of pop and a bath in one of the public facilities.

Or a bed in a packing case, sharing it with friends on nights in Paris, which even now are beginning to chill with autumn's coming.

(September 29, 1980.)

Voilà! A secret revealed

Paris. As we all stand on the brink of whatever it is we're standing on the brink of, let me offer a pleasant distraction that may pass the time more tastefully.

It's the secret formula for the way the French really make their fabulous mayonnaise.

Why this discovery has escaped other chow hounds, gourmets, gourmands, gluttons and epicures all these decades is one of modern civilization's riddles.

Where were those astute and learned food experts who came to whisk the techniques and discoveries from the Paul Bocuses, the Fernand Points and Cesar Ritz?

Where was Julia Child?

To have written, taught and promoted everything French in cooking and left out the prime secret of how you make mayonnaise is shameful.

I pried the secret loose quite by accident one evening last week when my wife and I were invited to dinner in Paris by some French friends, and I got into a discussion about food with a woman, a native of Scotland married to a Frenchman for many years.

She inquired about our meals so far in Paris and I waxed eloquently about the mayonnaise.

"How do they do it?" I said.

"It's so simple, it's preposterous that the French cooks and chefs have been playing coy with the recipe all these years," she said. "You use a silver spoon to whip the stuff. And you don't use any vinegar or any lemon juice."

The recipe, as she gave it, was this:

Break one, two or more egg yolks into any kind of a bowl. The number of eggs will depend upon how much mayonnaise you wish to make. But the French seldom make a lot at one time.

Add strong Dijon mustard to taste.

Then drizzle any kind of salad oil (your choice) into the bowl, stirring rapidly with a silver teaspoon or tablespoon. Do not use a whisk. Don't cheat by trying spoons made of pewter, silver plate, stainless steel or some other alloy.

"It has to be a silver spoon," she said.

No vinegar or lemon juice?

"NO!"

Never vinegar—and if you must, use only a few drops of lemon juice.

That's all there is to it. Beat, stir, whip that blend of egg yolk, oil and mustard with your silver spoon, adding oil until you get the consistency of mayonnaise you prefer.

"But you have to use a silver spoon," she said. "And if you haven't got one, call any of the Hunt brothers or borrow one from your more affluent neighbor. Better yet, buy one as a cooking utensil."

"I don't know," she said, "what there is about it, what the catalysts are, but that's how the French chefs and cooks really make their mayonnaise."

"It's so darned easy and everybody has made such a big deal out of it."

I thanked the woman kindly, memorized my notes and burned them up.

Travel does have its rewards.

Oh, by the way, I haven't tried the recipe yet.

But if it works I wouldn't, in all modesty, be adverse to being known in history as "the person who brought the secret of real French mayonnaise to America."

If it doesn't work, don't call me. I'll call you.

(September 15, 1980.)

City's St. Joseph sisters have strong link with France

Le Puy-en-Velay, France. We crossed the courtyard and rang the bell at No.19, Place Meurice, an almost hidden cul de sac in the old city. And just as another deluge of rain began falling, the door opened and a smiling nun hurried us into the grand foyer, shutting the heavy door against the breaking storm. As she led us to the reception parlour—"yes, we were expected"—I had to think that it was a long time and a long way from 1990 Randolph Ave. and the provincial house of the Sisters of St. Joseph of Carondelet.

Yet here is where the order of St. Joseph nuns was founded in 1651 and we were about to be treated to a gracious tour of the "motherhouse of them all."

Our hostess was the archivist, Sister Marie de la Tuircite. Along the way we picked up Sister St. Paule le Gabrielle, who made the coffee we drank later as the four of us sat around a refectory table, exchanging pleasantries about our-selves, about them and about the St. Joseph sisters we know back in St. Paul, including our close friends—Sisters Mary Henry Nachtsheim, Marie Philipe and Ann Thomasine Sampson.

Sister Marie pointed to the oil painting of the St. Joseph's tree—from the first seedling to the branch at St. Louis and Carondelet, which grew all the way to St. Paul in 1851.

And we listened as she spoke while we toured the vast convent, school and headquarters.

In the small but inspiring Romanesque chapel we recalled the story of how it happened.

In the late 1640s there was a group of girls who wished to form a community of women to do God's work, to comfort and treat the sick, help the poor and orphans, promote social justice and to visit, console and help, if possible, those in prisons. Educating the people so they could live fuller lives, was another mission.

The French Revolution took its toll on the order. Five were executed. Mother St. John Fontbonne, the superior, was spared by the fall of Robespierre, and she went on to reform the order in Lyons.

That tiny group, the acorn, grew to begin furnishing nuns for the pioneering of America in 1836.

Bishops and priests would write and say, "We need just the kinds of nuns you are—bringing culture and civiliza-tion, help for the sick and learning for the ignorant."

Translated, that has meant hospitals, schools, colleges and orphanages.

Through the decades very few St. Joseph's sisters from the St. Paul province have come back home here.

One who did, in 1969, was Sister Mary Henry of the College of St. Catherine French Department and International Studies program. She and several other nuns from around the Western world returned to find their roots at the request of Pope John.

"We found that our goals and sisters had not changed from the beginning," Sister Mary Henry told us before we left for France.

When we spoke of those things this afternoon over coffee and cookies to Sisters Marie and Paule, they nodded and said, "This is true of us all."

It was getting late in the afternoon, and the rain and mist were still enveloping the city. We had a drive through hill country to take.

Sister Marie escorted us to the edge of the convent courtyard and waved us goodbye.

"Send me a copy of anything you publish," she said.

"And don't forget who made the coffee," Sister Paule called out.

(October 13, 1981.)

Magnificent Marseille

Marseille, France. We came up out of Cassis in the morning and crossed the mountain-like Grand Corniche, zig-zagging in our rented car across the backbone of these topographical spines. Then we were over the hump and spread out below was Marseille.

The Mediterranean to the left was blue, the city sprawled in the sunlight, the spokes of the broad boulevards like airport runways: city of intrigue, fact and fiction, setting for so many recent TV and movie films, the producers' favorite stage.

"Set it in Marseille and we'll write the script to fit."

But always write a mystery, with high-speed chases through winding, bending narrow waterfront streets and alleys, two men hunched over a sidewalk café table, plotting, while the inspector lurks in the shadows of a doorway across the street.

This was the city, too, that became an exit for hundreds of refugees from Germany who were squeezed out of the port on the "last ships to freedom" in World War II. They included important writers, musicians, artists, philosophers, diplomats.

In dirty little cafés and sleazy hotels deals were made, fake passports arranged. Then, while foghorns moaned in the harbor and mist glazed the cobblestones, furtive packets of people boarded rusty, old boats for New York, Boston, Liverpool. And sometimes they never made it. A gun fired in the dark, a body floating in the harbor.

Suddenly, we are part of that city. The car has spiraled down and hurled itself into the midst of wide, wide Boulevard Michelet, four lanes for cars, greenery in the middle and two outer lanes for buses. The boulevard runs straight as an arrow.

We nose into the traffic, zip across one square, then into Rue de Rome and all at once the boulevard bottlenecks and we are in the heart of old Marseille, inching along in the biggest, noisiest, smelliest traffic jam imaginable. And on either sidewalk an immensity of humanity that is unbelievable. In the heat, the body odor seems to fill the cavernous streets.

St. Paul at high noon on payday is a ghost town by comparison. We feel trapped. Finally, the car sort of spews across majestic Boulevard Canebière and we rise up toward a version of the Arc de Triomphe.

A half-hour later, having entrusted our car to its rental owners, we are part of that maelstrom of on foot-Arabs, Turks, Iranians, Greeks, Orientals, Muslims. A polyglot seething, talking, shouting, laughing.

Food stands parked between sidewalk and street sell Pain Baignat (Riviera-style Hoagies with tuna and anchovies), hamburgers stuffed into long, crusty French rolls and topped by French fries. This is the noon hour and the fast food carts run like assembly lines.

Watch your feet. Every dog in France has promenaded on the sidewalks of Marseille today. Flies hover, then spiral off the droppings to the pan of raw hamburger patties on the food cart counter.

The waterfront is hot, muggy. Old hotels stand alongside new, modern apartment houses, with balconies where tenants have views heaven will be hard pressed to surpass.

Cafés string out along the sunshine side of the port. We find a table outdoors on the corner and have lunch and watch the crowds. Now, we are spectators.

The shady side of the port is for harbor people, the patrons of the "happy voyagers" bar, whose clientele are right out of a Captain Kidd scene.

Here are the warehouses, shipping company headquarters, storage sheds from whose barrels and boxes, bales, kegs and containers waft aromas of adventure out of their cool, musty depths.

Trucks back and throttle. Tugs tear across the harbor from freighter to freighter.

By late afternoon we have gone to Gare St. Charles and boarded "Le Mistral" streamliner for Paris.

A lavishly dressed African princess (it was whispered), bejeweled, tinkling with bracelets and turban-crowned, is in our car.

You expect this when you leave Marseille.

(September 22, 1980.)

Filling in porcelain's past

Limoges, France. It was a sentimental quest with a strange ending on the floor of a modern office building on Rue du Général Cérez, a tiny street in this porcelain capital of France.

We had come in search of M. Redon, maker of fine Limoges china, because of a purchase made more than 60 years ago.

The story begins in 1919 in Chicago. My wife's father and mother, newly married, had taken a trip to Chicago.

It was at Marshall Field and Co. on Chicago's State Street that they bought their china—fine Limoges, made by the factory of M. Redon.

Both of my wife's parents are dead. And my wife, an only child, inherited their Limoges china set. Which, as so much of it does, spends more time gathering dust in a top cupboard than serving food.

When we planned this trip to France my wife thought it would be fun to find the factory that made her heirloom china and see whether they could match a piece or two.

There are, we discovered, 41 porcelain factories in Limoges, among them such prestigious places as Haviland, founded in 1842; A. Reynaud and Co., circa 1856; and I Bernardaud, 1863.

Porcelain shops are, in fact, as popular and numerous in Limoges as McDonald's hamburger restaurants are in America. Porcelain is as common as Tupperware.

We also discovered that the quality of all Limoges hard clay porcelain is on an almost equal plane. Namedroppers may prefer Haviland and Reynaud as art fanciers do "name" painters. But it's the same Kaolin clay being used by everybody, and similar glazing processes. The style and designs, however, are varied and the extent to which handcrafting still is employed makes the difference.

M. Redon began making porcelain in Limoges in 1862 and was among the most fashionable and popular of china makers. At some time or other, he merged with a factory named Gibus and they made porcelain until 1928.

Then, for reasons we could not learn, the factory closed and the last pieces were sold by 1938.

Perhaps, as almost happened with the porcelain empire of David Haviland, the family died out and no one was willing to carry on the business. Haviland, fortunately, found successors to continue and today the firm of Haviland and Robert Haviland and C. Parlon are busy filling china closets around the world.

We left the offices of the Porcelain Association a little dejected. The only thing that buoyed our spirits was a suggestion by the directoress that Redon porcelain was becoming more valuable as the years passed because of its limited quantity and age.

On a hunch, we walked over to the Porcelain Museum and began to look at porcelain from Limoges through its 138-year history.

I will never know what made us stop, suddenly, in front of one glassed-in show window and read the name of the firm which had made the porcelain on display.

There it was: "M. Redon, 1868."

We found more Redon porcelain in the museum and some during the Gibus-Redon era. As late as 1925. That would have been somewhat in the period when my mother-in-law got hers.

Although Redon worked in many styles, what we saw was not too dissimilar to the design we have in St. Paul.

We walked out of the museum feeling almost as if our mission had been accomplished. At least we knew that Grandma's Limoges porcelain had a worthy and noble heritage.

She had made a good choice.

(September 17, 1980.)

French village remains quiet about its important history

Le Chambon-sur-Lignon, France. I have saved our visit to Le Chambon for the end of these travels because it can't be told in a single column. I will try in three, but even then, you will get only a brief look at the village and how it was during World War II when it achieved some immortality and what it is like now.

On the last night of our stay, a motorcycle club of the region celebrated its monthly dinner meeting in the Hotel

Central, where we were staying. I doubt that any of the members, in their 20s and 30s, had even the slightest recollections of how their families had saved thousands of Jews and other refugees from the Nazis between 1942 and VE Day in 1945.

Nobody really knows how many paused, lived or passed through Le Chambon, because nobody is sure how many families in the protestant village were part of this vast underground railroad to safety and freedom.

"It was the best-kept secret of the entire war, and still is. Otherwise, it couldn't have succeeded," said Lesley Maber, English-born retired professor at Chambon's Cevenol College.

"To call a rally in a hall and announce what we were doing, to even mention it on the street, or in a store, or church would have been fatal. The village would have been massacred by the Germans as they massacred others in this area of Vichy-Occupied France.

"Of course the Vichy authorities and Germans suspected what was going on. But they never could put a finger on it, never get evidence, never find anyone," she said.

Maber was our Chambon connection. She was asked to help us by Magda Trocmé, whose late husband, Huguenot pastor André Trocmé, was one of the men finally sent to a concentration camp near Limoges and later released. Trocmé's daughter, Nelly Blackburn, teaches French at Blake School in Hopkins. Blackburn was a teenager in Le Chambon during those years. She had helped us meet "our connection."

"Once a unit of Gendarmes came here to make a determined search," Maber said. "I sort of chided one for turning on his own countrymen and women. He said, "Look, if we hadn't come, the German SS or Gestapo would have." The Gendarmes made what looked like a diligent hunt, masking a feigned effectiveness, then left empty-handed.

"Do you know that except for a memorial monument put up across from the Temple (the Huguenot hall) there is no tangible record in this village that anything ever happened out of the ordinary?" Maber said.

And then there is the bestseller book, *Lest Innocent Blood be Shed*, by American scholar and philosopher Philip Hallie. The book has made Le Chambon a part of the bigger Holocaust story, and has also embarrassed the village with ensuing fame.

"But our whole purpose was to save lives without bloodshed," Maber said, as we talked at the hotel during our first evening in the village.

"We are essentially a village of French Huguenots. We believe in peace and reconciliation, not war."

She spoke of the refugees coming out of the woods and forest, skirting the road from Valence or Le Puy or Tence. In a sense, Le Chambon is a natural refuge—high in the mountainous hills of the Massif Central with thick woods, streams, winding and narrow roads.

"They knew (via the grapevine) where a room was ready, a basement niche, an attic. They stayed, took the provisions left for them and next morning might be gone. Who knew who had been sleeping in your house?"

"You know, there were very few Catholics in Le Chambon in those years. Ecumenicism had not yet begun. It wasn't until recently we found out that Catholic families had been among the most active saving lives.

"I should have known. Once, I asked the priest whether he might lend me a cassock. I didn't say why. He didn't ask.

But he refused. He said: 'You know, priests wearing cassocks are the first people the Germans search at railroad stations and on the streets.' I got the message."
(October 26, 1981.)

Village's fragile 'little Saint' still radiates inner courage

Le Chambon-sur-Lignon, France. "What we did was done naturally," said the woman sitting across from me. It was a refrain I kept hearing.

"It all began for me one day in 1942 when Pastor (André) Trocmé (of the Huguenot Temple) came to me and said that since I had a boarding house, perhaps I could take a few people he would send. It was like that. He didn't say they would be Jewish refugees from France or other countries. It was always like that. Nobody ever told anybody more than you should know."

The words and voice belonged to Mme. Gabrielle Barraud, one of the active survivors of Chambon's rescue of Jews during World War II.

It was our first afternoon here and English-speaking guide Lesley Maber had picked us up at the hotel and taken us to her comfortable, English-style cottage with woods and garden below the house. A wood stove glowed. Teacups had just been put out.

"I have just been entertaining Mme. Barraud, our 'Little Saint' of the village," said Lesley. "She speaks some English."

Mme. Barraud, tiny, fragile-looking deceptively hiding steel courage, was 88 on her last birthday. Her voice is strong, her eyes twinkle. She seldom mentions her own tragedies in the war.

Later she took us to that boarding house, now the picturesque, little Hotel Beau Soleil, on the edge of the village, perched on a ledge. Thirty-eight years ago, it was a key stop on the Jewish underground railroad that led to Switzerland and Spain. As we drove and as she led us through the familiar rooms, she talked of those days:

"I remember one day in late November of 1942. It had snowed terribly. The drifts were piled up around the front door, so nobody could go out. The boys always went out the rear door, down below, the basement door. I had three foreign Jewish boys who had just come. We were all in the dining room, getting ready for supper when I looked outside and saw six Gestapo men in front.

"The three Jewish boys got scared. They wanted to run out the back door. I said, 'No, we all stay right here in the dining room, boys, and act as if you are regular boarders, and students at the college. Don't do a thing.'

"The Gestapo came in, searched the house, looked in casually at the boys busy with their homework, setting the table, shook their heads and left.

"Now, if, those three Jewish boys had made a run for it, it would have been too bad for them and us. You see, that was how we handled things, that was normal living for us for almost three years."

"Can I say something?" Lesley chimed in. "Your Nelly Blackburn in the Twin Cities. She was a Girl Guide and I had the Girl Guides go out into the woods and along the paths that led to and from Le Puy and toward Valence ostensibly on hikes to earn what you call merit badges. Actually, they came back with excellent maps we could furnish the refugees."

I heard later that Mme. Barraud spends her days visiting the sick and the elderly in the nursing home, never missing her rounds. That's why they call her the "Little Saint."

She had one last story to tell before we said goodbye.

"I had a Jewish rabbi living in a bare room. A secret place. He practiced his faith and held services for the others, always clandestinely. One day we had to get him out of the village in a hurry, because of a report of danger. As he left, he handed me a little memento and on it he had written:

"'Because you have done it unto us, the least of these, you have done it unto Me.'

"Imagine, a Jewish rabbi leaving with the word of Jesus!" (October 27, 1981.)

Old man remembers helping during World War II

Le Chambon-sur-Lignon, France. The little train no longer runs from Le Chambon, except on summer excursions. But one day in 1944 it took three "musketeers" off to a concentration camp near Limoges.

The three were Pastor André Trocmé, Eduard Theis, director of Cevenol College, and Roger Darcissac, headmaster of the village school.

(Cevenol College, founded in 1940 by Trocmé and Theis, is actually a Huguenot-oriented academy for boys and girls ages 8 to 18 who come from all over the world except Russia and Iron Curtain countries. They study the basics, lots of languages and a philosophy of peace and reconciliation. Fully accredited by the French government, it flourishes today with a campus of buildings in the woods. It played a role in that walk to the train.)

The scene that day at the train, as the three men walked slowly through the village, carrying their suitcases and guarded by policemen, is like a faded tintype. The people stood on the curbs, silently, furtively handing the three men food, socks, underwear and books, and forming prayers on their lips.

Pastor Trocmé is dead now. His wife, Magda, tours the world on behalf of fellowship and reconciliation. She lives in Paris some of the time. Theis is in a home for the aged in Valence. Darcissac lives in a small apartment in a house overlooking the Lignon. He is 83 and not well.

It was Sunday when we saw him there, still in his pajamas and bathrobe, apologizing for his attire. On his lap he had souvenirs to jog his memory: a photo album of life in the concentration camp during the month the three men were interrogated, threatened and finally released. They never betrayed the secret of Le Chambon: the underground railroad that shuttled Jews to safety beyond the Nazi-occupied areas of Europe.

"I smuggled the camera inside. The French and Germans were horrified later when they found out.

"You know, we had never known any of us were involved so deeply," Darcissac said of his other two friends. "It was a surprise to all of us that morning when they arrested and marched us down to the train. All I ever knew was that some mornings in my school, I would find French or foreign Jewish boys. Then one day they would be gone and new faces appeared.

"Oh, once in awhile Trocmé would come to the house and ask whether it was all right to enroll outsiders. We covered up their being Jewish as best we could. We succeeded. But the

French authorities and German SS, the commander in Le Puy, they had to make examples of somebody here in the village. Once we got to the concentration camp, then we began comparing notes and became close friends. But even there, of course, it was all very secret, our conversations."

Darcissac was released first. He returned to the school and the job he had held. Trocmé went to Switzerland. Theis left the village and later was reported to have become a "passeur," a man who passed the refugees from Occupied France into Switzerland through the Alps.

The old man looked out of the window at the bright, blue sky after two days of rain. He said it again:

"What we did we did naturally. It was what anybody else would have done." But not everyone else did.

(October 28, 1981.)

Meet king of world chefs

Lyon, France. Twelve miles up the Saone River from Lyon, the words "Paul Bocuse" seem to hang in the evening sky in garish, green neon. They mark the restaurant palace of the self-proclaimed king ("I am the greatest") of the world's chefs and restauranteurs.

Twice daily, at noon and night, the great man's minions, directed by him (when he isn't bucketing around the globe on culinary missions), serve memorable meals to pilgrims of dining who have come to pay homage to the co-author of modern French cooking in his celebrated culinary castle. They have reserved their tables as much as four and five months ahead. We did it by letter last April. The king himself signed our confirmation.

Paul Bocuse welcomes guests to his famous restaurant in a mural painted by artists from La Cité de la Création in 1993.

The setting is a royal blend of tables with fresh pink roses, matching pink candles in candelabras, lighted as dusk falls over the valley and the restaurant lights are dimmed for full effect. Crystal is everywhere, and the walls are hung with an awful mismatching of paintings and sculptures, kitschy figures alongside altarpieces, side by side with religious statues. The staff overwhelmed us with service and smiles. There were the maitre d', the captain of waiters and a young woman, probably Bocuse's daughter, who met us at the entrance. Our table in a cozy corner of the solarium was the scene of lavish Bocuse cooking.

Hardly have the chairs been pushed under the table when the wine waiter appears with a silver pitcher of Bocuse's favorite aperitif: white wine with Cassis liqueur and raspberry sauce. He departs in favor of our waiter, who proffers a slice of country pâté in a pastry shell. So far everything is "on the house."

You start paying when the waiter reappears to take your order and the sommelier jots down your wine selections.

And I want to say at the outset that there is no way that words can adequately describe the wonders of flavor and preparation.

My choices that night:

Generous slices of fresh, raw, pink salmon with a dill béarnaise sauce; a fish course of Loup (sea bass) with lobster mousse en croute, shaped like a fish; then the entrée of Supreme de volaille de Bresse aux foie d'oie and truffle (slices of chicken breast baked and served with goose liver pâté and covered with slices of morel (wild, forest mushrooms) sautéed in butter.

All of these were Bocuse favorites, and I endeared myself to everybody, including the dishwasher, by ordering them.

By then I was ready to call for the reserves, but there was still the big tray of French and Swiss and Dutch cheeses (not even the remarkable Raess market on St. Clair Avenue has them). Then came the plate of petit fours, followed by sorbet drenched with more Cassis and raspberry syrup and, finally, coffee.

My wife, "the little sparrow," was more discreet. She made do with a pike mousse covered with a hollandaise-type sauce, skipped the fish course to preserve her size 10 clothes and went right onto the main course, slices of veal in a béarnaise-type sauce with morels sautéed in garlic butter. She also did the cheese bit, a strawberry tart and the petit fours plus coffee.

Bocuse, I suspect, is being subsidized by the sugar and chocolate industries.

The great man was not there to knight us. He had left that morning for Los Angeles, our waiter told us.

The wines we drank were a half bottle of white and half bottle of Beaujolais, both with Bocuse labels.

This was our big splurge of the trip, and the tab was under $90 for two, an amazing bargain compared with what you pay for much less quality and presentation in almost any other top-drawer place in the Western world. Thanks be to the French price freeze and the 7 franc dollar.

Three hours had passed by now and the cab ride back to our hotel in Lyon was superfluous. We should have jogged. (September 29, 1982.)

Village offers glimpse of Shangri-La

Collioure, France. Sometime more than 80 years ago, the painters Derain, Braque and Matisse discovered this tiny French village on the Mediterranean coast near the Spanish border and launched an art movement known as "Fauvism."

In their wake came other artists with household names—Dali, Chagall, Vlaminck and Picasso.

They created an aura and fame for Collioure that brings artists and people like us here to see what they saw and painted, and to savor the tranquil, calm life they found so attractive. It also was a chance to live with these villagers, who are so much like their neighbors in Catalonia, just across the Spanish border.

Were any of the "Fathers of Fauvism" able to come back now, they would find the stage virtually unspoiled by the modernism of high rises, condominiums and skyscraping resort hotels. There are none of these here.

With great wisdom, Collioure's devotees have made the village a national monument, and any changes in building or architecture are forbidden. The pink-and-rose-painted stucco houses with red tiled roofs in the Spanish-Catalan mode still drape the hills. The massive fortress walls, the famed lighthouse tower and 11th-century château protect this side of paradise from the sound and fury of the outside world.

There is a sort of Moorish, medieval ambiance. A French Foreign Legion setting is enhanced by the military Caserne standing on the lofty heights behind the village, still a French army post. From behind the ramparts each morning revéille sounds, followed by the playing of the Marseillaise. And at 7 p.m. each day, retreat is held, the French tri-color lowered against the setting sun.

From our balcony window on the fourth floor of the little Boramar Hotel, we can see the harbor's many moods and dramas and all the antiquities that so charmed the painters and still do.

On the floor below us, an artist works each morning at his easel, painting the harbor, the château, lighthouse and village landscape. He spends the hot afternoons on the beach, as we did, lazing in the sun, swimming in the Mediterranean.

Alas, I fear his painting will not match the masterpiece Paul Signac did of the same tower, harbor and revetments, which now hangs in the Metropolitan Museum in New York City.

The harbors, the beaches and windy, narrow streets on a Sunday afternoon in July are a montage of people of all dress and styles. Scantily clad—the women often topless—people of all shapes and sizes loll on the beach. They come in family lots from nearby towns and cities. They pitch colorful umbrellas, unfold chairs and read or sleep; they swim and windsurf and go scuba diving. They relax under shady tree bowers of out-door cafés, they fill boutiques and shops. Then at dusk, when the floodlights turn the 17th-century Baroque church of St. Mary Madeleine and the Château Royal into an old rose tint, the Sunday visitors stream homeward, leaving the charm to the tourists and natives to appreciate.

Then we come out and watch the men play at boules (a game similar to bowling), and at about 8 p.m. we begin the search for the right restaurant. Always, we eat the same things—the famed fish soup, the delicious soup with crou-tons topped with garlic-and red-pepper-flavored mayon-naise, the Catalan-styled fish or chicken immersed in spicy tomato-based sauces.

Nights run into midnight. One night, we go to a class to learn the folk dance Sardana in a hot, old gymnasium. We are all feet and little else, but somehow our teachers get us coor-dinated. The entire class turns out a few nights later in the plaza to dance to a nine-piece band, and it's as if we'd lived there all our lives. Our new friends are fellow classmates.

On another evening, we sit under the stars in the court-yard of the Château Royal and listen to a Brazilian-Andes musical group play haunting music on guitars and other stringed instruments.

We stroll streets lighted only by lanterns, hearing the lively sounds of families eating and laughing behind the closed wooden shutters of their curbside houses.

It all comes together very easily, all the centuries blending into a slow-motion roll of time, like the waves of the tide washing over the beaches, all the scenes mixing into a grand painting of a timeless village you leave with deep regret. We have had a glimpse of Shangri-La.
(July 25, 1983.)

Festival season brings crowds to south France

Avignon, France. Paris' Gare de Lyon terminal was hot and humid when we left it by fast TGV train; our rented car was smoldering in the sun outside the Avignon station. Ten minutes later, we were splashing in the cool, huge, bluewater swimming pool of an enchanted, shaded château hotel called Le Prieuré (Priory).

It was our introduction to French summer "festival time" and Jacques and Marie France Mille's adaptation of what a Catholic cardinal named Arnaud built in 1322 in the tiny village of Villeneuve-lès-Avignon, just across the Rhone from Avignon. The Popes didn't have room for him in their own palaces, so he said "to heck with that" and built his own.

We were not alone.

When June ends and July and August come to France, entertainers, show troupes, acting companies, opera singers, orchestras and motion picture booking; agencies all go south for myriad festivals. Promoters and cultural societies round up the great opera stars, the best symphonies and legitimate theater casts and put on nightly performances, week after week, into early September.

From Avignon and Orange to Aix-en-Provence and Arles, from Marseille to Nice, Cannes to St. Tropez there are festivals. Few villages or towns escape the festival scene, and special editions of newspapers and magazines spell out the bills of fare.

Old cathedrals, Roman ruins, open air amphitheaters and historic buildings are used for poetry readings, jazz concerts, choirs, medieval plays, sound and light shows. You can stand on the ramparts of a tower near the hotel on Bastille Day night and watch fireworks rocketing out over the palace of the popes in Avignon.

There are 140 festivals this summer in southern France.

One night it was a jazz festival in the courtyard of the palace of the popes in Avignon; another evening we just walked around the corner into the center of an old fortress and heard a rare concert by Byzantine chanters from Athens.

Ariane Mnouchkine, rising young producer-director from New York City, was doing Shakespeare's "Richard II" in Avignon. The cast wore Japanese facemasks. But the whipped cream on the festival cake came in nearby Orange, where one evening we joined 10,000 opera-goers for a performance of "Don Carlos," starring such opera household names as Montserrat Caballe, Simon Estes and Grace Bumbry.

It was the Superbowl of the French summer festival season, held in an old Roman theater built in the days of the Empire, the stage still mostly intact, the seats hard stone, softened by cushions thoughtfully provided by our hotel-keeper, M. Mille.

The scene outside the theater was bedlam, motorists searching for parking space and crowds milling about, trying to buy tickets from us.

We lucked out with a cab driver, who took us to a charming hillside restaurant, then brought us back in time for the 10 p.m. opera start. It lasted until 1:30 a.m., and there wasn't a drooping eyelid in the crowd. The cheers at the end would rouse the envy of a Vikings football team after a victory.

On another evening, we saw a seldom-heard Mozart opera, "La Finta Giardiniera," in another open-air museum theater in Aix-en-Provence, 70 miles from Avignon. Four thousand people packed into this theater under the stars.

In between concerts and operas, we regrouped at the Prieuré, whose air-conditioned medieval rooms, bon vivantism, joie de vivre and hospitality were matched by the cool arbors, riotous flower beds and meals on the patio that rate a Michelin one-star.

It was Jacques Mille's father, Roger, who acquired one end of the old priory in 1944 and, little by little, with the help of his son, turned it into one of France's most celebrated hostelries. Jacques and Marie France are carrying on the tradition, adding here and there the creature comforts of 1984 without losing any of the 14th-century style.

Few hotelkeepers spend as much time with their guests as the Milles, who seemingly never sleep. A napkin out of place, a stray crumb on a tablecloth, a missing knife are major crises for them.

When festival season is over, the Prieuré closes down for four winter months for refurbishing.

"The cardinals, bishops and priests who lived here established living standards that were fairly lavish for their day," says Jacques. "I suspect they enjoyed everything we do now—food, quarters and even a pool of sorts."

Including the occasional gorgeous topless French woman sitting at the pool?
(August 3, 1984.)

Pair of moving and movable picnics

Laval, Normandy, France. We could hardly get to Europe fast enough to create those roadside picnic lunches.

Our first two may have been the keepers for the memory album, but for strangely different reasons.

The fun of picnicking in Europe is going from shop to shop in the cities and towns, buying the "Fixings."

The morning we left Frankfurt, Germany, we were out on the Kaiser Strasse mall by 8 a.m., buying hot, fresh croissants here, a pair of steamed bratwurst there at a stall; a fresh, big ripe tomato and two ripe peaches at a fruit market; a stick of smoked landjaeger sausage and a few ounces of griessenschmalz with several slices of Schinken bread; then a bottle of Durkheimer light red wine, a pair of filbert-chocolate cookies and we were in business.

The baker was just bringing in the rolls and croissants when we got to the bäckerei. The aromas are wonderful even to recall.

We competed at the counters with thousands of Frankfurters, pouring off commuter trains at the Hauptbahnhof (railroad station) at the end of the mall.

But it was pleasant, smiling jostling for position. They went to work with their "picnics." We took to the open highways and four hours later, just inside France, at a wayside filling station-café-picnic ground, we decided to picnic.

The site was filled with natural beauty, trees, pines, shade, grass. The day was warm, still and sunny. The food was everything we hoped it would taste like.

But we reckoned without patches of clover and les abeilles (bees) which found my wife first, then our lunch and it became like one of those nightmare movies where the birds and bees take over the world.

Only here they took over our lunch. I managed to finish mine, by sort of jogging around the grounds and waving one hand in an arc. Like a windmill.

My wife must have seemed sweeter. The bees literally followed the food into her mouth. Observers from nearby watched her do a fast disco, blended with a whirling ballet step.

We capitulated. And went into the wayside café for coffee au lait. My wife finished her lunch somewhere on the AutoRoute to Metz. We got rid of the last bee near Compiegne of World War I history and buried it without honors.

Next morning we were up and out in a cool, clear, fresh morning in the downtown streets of Beauvais, just as the shops opened and before the sudsy water had dried on the ancient stone sidewalks, just scrubbed by fussy entrepreneurs.

People were beginning to carry out the long, thin, golden loaves of crusty French bread, shouldering it like muskets or fishing rods.

We chose two more fresh, flaky, hot croissants in the boulangerie, then half dozen slices of boudin noir (blood sausage) and a small mound of rillettes, cooked pork and seasoning, freshly minced and ground. A specialty of Normandy.

And it was just after an hour in artist Claude Monet's garden at Giverny that we found a wayside of our own along the same stream that runs through his lily pad garden with the Japanese bridge.

Our table was an old, long abandoned railroad bridge over the narrow stream—perhaps 10 feet long.

There we spread everything out on the rotting timbers, covered by our newspapers. No people sounds broke the reverie. We sat long into the noon hour, savoring all we ate. Lazing in the sun and listening to the ripple of the water over rocks.

Our benches were railroad ties and our "patio," the rusting steel plates.

The only intrusion was by a young bicyclist who asked the way to a restaurant, unfortunately after we had eaten. So we couldn't share.

We have written it down in our "Trip Notes" as "Lunch near Monet's Garden. No bees."

(September 8, 1979.)

Exploring Europe

Monsters, Pardons, wine festivals—every airplane, train, automobile or ferry boat led us to new adventures, some planned, some unexpected. All enriched our understanding of other people and places and our enthusiasm for travel experiences.

A night of Loch Ness waiting in Monsterland

Drumnadrochit, on Loch Ness, Scotland. Even if you never see the Loch Ness monster, the Drumnadrochit Hotel "where the monster plays in the bay, so they say," is worth the trip.

Built in 1882 of charcoal granite, on a promontory commanding a view of both Loch and valley, the three-story, gabled inn has been Monster Expedition Headquarters ever since it greeted the first guest almost a century ago.

The staff may have changed several times, but not the furnishings, the dignity and the style of life.

Nor has the Drumnadrochit ever relinquished its zest for a good Loch Ness monster story or search party.

The first travelers and monster aficionados arrived by Loch steamer in the 1880s and transferred to coaches—hence its name as a coaching inn of yore. In 1977, the modern versions of the same people come by motor car and coach.

170

And the Grant family, who fought at Culloden in 1746, managed to salvage one descendant who opened the inn. The present "Laird" of the hotel and surrounding flower and kitchen gardens is Ronnie A. Bremner, who is considered the custodian of Loch Ness lore and presides in both dining room and hotel pub wearing the Bremner kilts.

We arrived at the hotel just after 5 p.m. on a warm, almost clear late August afternoon, pausing near Castle Urquhart across the bay from the hotel to watch the monster watchers who gather from sunup to sundown, year after year. Many faithful watchers pitch tents nearby. We saw nothing in the water except horrendous white caps.

The Drumnadrochit Hotel is a far more comfortable way to wait than tenting and it was nearly empty. The great lounge with heavy chairs and tables, the frescoed ceilings and trimmed wainscoting is more like a museum, or a stage waiting for something to happen, like the arrival of Queen Victoria.

Our room, a spacious abode fronting the bay, was comfortably old-Scotland as certainly was the thin, leather-faced man, in black visored cap and black suit, waiting at the front door.

Not for us, he explained, but for the coach bringing the 37 tourists who would spend the night. He was, he explained, actually the gardener and would we step outside after dinner to see his handiwork and also the spring of pure, clear cold water said to have been blessed by St. Columba?

The coach rolled up just then and suddenly the hotel was filled with people, languages and luggage. It was, said the winsome hostess, like "last summer."

Last summer was when *National Geographic* and the big, skeptical newspapers all sent staffmen to Drumnadrochit to observe the scientific work being done to locate the monster.

Dr. Robert H. Rines of Boston and the Academy of Applied Science was in more or less command by virtue of a photograph he took in 1972 below the Loch surface showing something in the shape of a fin.

That turned the hotel pub into a veritable bedlam night after night as the locals came to hear the latest results of the underwater scientific probing and spin a few monstrous tales themselves. They brought their pipes to play and wore kilts and had a jolly go at it.

All the while, the lovely Fiona drew pints and half pints of lager behind the bar and got her name in the June issue of *National Geographic*, which miffed slightly the lovely Cheryl, who had replaced the lovely Fiona. But I promised I would put her name in my column and she brightened up considerably.

Cooking at the Drumnadrochit is one of those reasons to stay here. That night we had honeydew melon and egg mayonnaise (with Mrs. Bremner's homemade mayonnaise), consomme Portuguese and fresh Loch Ness salmon mayonnaise.

After dinner coffee is served in the lounge as it is everywhere in Scottish hotels. We took a corner table in one of the window bays so we could look out across the lounge at the guests cozily sipping the steaming brew and chatting about the day's events. Others went strolling through the gardens in the dusk to get their "constitutional."

It was, I suppose, like similar occasions everywhere the British Empire went—thoroughly dull – and it needed only a Somerset Maugham or Rudyard Kipling to finish it properly. (September 9, 1977.)

Mère Poulard's famous omelettes

Mont St. Michel, Normandy, France. If the Archangel Michael inspired the construction of the Abbey of Mont St. Michel as one of the Seven Wonders of the World, a woman named Annette Poulard gave this big rock a second wonder called L'Omelette de Mme. Poulard.

Mother Poulard did her stuff at the end of the last century creating fluffy, exquisite omelettes by holding her beaten eggs over an open-hearth fire of oak logs in a long handled pan.

Her tiny restaurant, near the entrance arch of Mont St. Michel, has become the Hotel-Restaurant de la Mère Poulard, a one star Michelin establishment, thanks in large part to Mother Poulard who, God rest her soul, has gone to her reward—hopefully a heaven filled with beaten eggs, waiting for her touch.

What she achieved has spread all up and down the narrow, winding main Mont St. Michel village street, so that no less than a dozen hotels and restaurants promote omelettes—not filled with anything, not hoked up, just plain omelettes.

But L'Hotel-Restaurant de la Mère Poulard is the citadel of omelettes just as the abbey above is for the Mont.

And in a special omelette kitchen between the lobby and streetside dining room each evening, young women dressed in long, black gowns as Mother Poulard always did, cook omelettes according to her recipe.

This she passed on to the present operators of the Inn, Monsieur and Madame Bernard Heyraud.

I not only had the pleasure of eating one of those omelettes during a stay in the hotel, but watched it cooked and then brought out the recipe.

Unfortunately, duplicating the modus operandi may be nigh impossible.

What it takes is a young man about 18, trained to whip in musical rhythm two eggs per person in a copper bowl. This he does with lightning wrist action for three minutes.

All the while, one of the young women has been melting butter in a tin-lined, long handled copper pan—holding it over a big log fire in a huge hearth.

Then she holds the pan near the bowl of beaten eggs and the young man pours the mixture into the already piping, sizzling hot, cooking pan.

She holds the pan over the fire, stirring with a fork all around the edges from time to time.

She also cooks the eggs slowly, taking them off the fire often so that the omelettes will rise like a soufflé. Now and then she dips the pan into the flame to brown the top of the cooking eggs.

When it is still partially frothy, she turns it out of the pan and folds the omelette over on a metal serving tray. It looks four inches high.

And a waiter in dinner jacket whips it to your table.

The secret, I suggest, after proper beating, is in removing the pan from the fire or heat often so it will rise and not adding a lot of junk. Just eggs. No more, no less.

The omelette is the piéce de rèsistance of the menu.

For salt-fed lamb at its best in Normandy, where it should be good, I'd go back to the Hotel du Chalet in Pontorson where we stayed the night before coming to Mont St. Michel.

That lamb was juicy, tender, a little pink and melted in the mouth, with just a touch of garlic-rosemary flavor.

Back at Mère Poulard, the desserts—especially the Coupes (ice creams with varied ingredients) rate a star.

The American egg board should award Mère Poulard a posthumous golden egg. More eggs are used in Mont St. Michel each day than in all of New York City, one enthusiast on the hotel staff told me.

And no mention is made anywhere about cholesterol or calories.

They just let it all hang out of an omelette pan. (September 15, 1978.)

Château-hopping with Joan of Arc

Loches, France. It was cool, clear and fresh as one of the melons on the outdoor stands across the street from our Hotel de France when we started our château-hopping day in the Greater Loire Valley.

Along the way we followed in Jeanne d'Arc's (Joan of Arc's) path and found the château where the setting was laid for the fairy tale "Sleeping Beauty." There were winding backcountry roads through farm hamlets, forests, vineyards where the great wines of the Loire begin in the golden sunshine.

Sometimes the landscape was a portrait of southern Minnesota's broad cornfields and other times the Minnesota River valley between Mankato and Belle Plaine. Our picnic hamper was replenished at the charcuterie and patisserie, the wine shop and the comestible store as we drove out of Loches.

First stop—one that few tourists ever make; Americans, never. An old man carrying a thin, long loaf of fresh French bread answered our inquiry at the edge of tiny St. Catherine de Fierbois, some 10 miles from Loches and said we were the first Americans he had met in 10 years.

Yet students of history miss the tall statue of Joan of Arc, in her familiar pose, flag of France in one hand, sword in the other. It stands in the center of tiny St. Catherine, a farm village of two streets.

It was here that she sent her emissaries to find a sword, lying behind the altar of the church because the "voices" had told her it would be there.

It would have, she said, five fleurs de lis on the hilt.

The emissaries came and on March 3, 1429, they found the sword exactly as Joan described it. This further convinced the Dauphin, later Charles VII, that Joan was indeed blessed of supernatural powers.

So the statue stands amid a small garden of brilliant flowers in front of the church where it all happened. And on a sunny, still, warm September morning in 1978, you can see it all again in your mind.

But not to tarry. For Chinon on the L'Indre awaits a dozen miles away and the formidable Chinon castle of ruins from the Middle Ages, where Joan of Arc was received by the Dauphin and her bedroom is on the tour route.

Here one can also buy, at myriad stands, the Chinon rouge (red) wines we never find in America and the stellar Vouvrays which we do at prices as high as the Chinon castle.

The noon chimes brought us down the hill to a riverside garden and "pique-nique" mall, where we spread our viands on a bench and joined dozens of other tourists in the French lunch tradition.

By early afternoon, we had passed the massive French atomic power plant near Chinon and gone from this symbol of modernity back into the romantic past of childhood and the legend of "Sleeping Beauty." Or, as the author Charles Perrault called it in French, "Belle au Bois Dormant."

The setting for this immortal story is the Château of L'Indre, a storybook-like castle of towers and turrets, on a hill looking into the L'Indre River valley.

Sleeping Beauty doesn't live there anymore, but most of the château is inhabited by the Marquis (Count) of Blacas and his family, long time residents who maintain an elegant cross-section of "life in a château" for tourists.

There was just enough time left in the afternoon to meander through the gardens and woods of L'Indre to the granddaddy of all châteaux, Chenonceau, residence of the most illustrious of the Grandes Dames of France, beginning with Catherine de' Medici, wife of Henry II and more recently Madame Dupin, grandmother of George Sand. Her restoration of this almost trite château in world photographs is now being done by the Meunier chocolate family. Chenonceau arches into the Cher River and towards sunset, with white swans rippling the water, it is indescribably magnificent.

One is prone to say, driving back through the setting sunlight of a perfect day toward Loches, that when you've seen one château, you've seen them all.

(September 22, 1978.)

Tale of a bill in a china shop

Quimper, Brittany, France. This is the city near the Brittany coast of France that is synonomous with Quimper ware china, distinctive painted patterns as cherished almost as Limoges, Staffordshire or Dresden china.

For those hundreds of Minnesotans—the figure is not exaggerated—who own or eat off of Quimper china, guard your settings and serving sets as you would your best silver. I have been to the well and it is gushing forth wares that might well be pure gold, silver or uranium.

And unless you merely want the pleasure and delight of seeing for yourself where it is fired, handpainted and sold, you might as well stay home and buy yours at any of the better shops in St. Paul or Minneapolis.

It may be cheaper, I'm sure it is if you buy here in quantity and want to ship home.

But even with the rude awakening had, our visit to HB-HENRIOT, at a corner of Place de la Cathedrale, in the very heart of downtown Quimper, was a goal reached.

This little shop, with its half dozen bustling staff, is the major retail outlet for "THE" HB-Henriot china of Quimper, which signature you see on the bottom of every piece of the Henriot factory's work.

Alas, for us, the occasion was far less than we had hoped or planned to bring back to fill out a modest breakfast set of Quimper ware, which began with a pair of egg cups I bought at Th'rice Cooking School and store on Grand Avenue for a wedding anniversary several years ago.

We walked over to the square from our hotel bright and early and a pleasant woman on the staff—when she heard we wanted to match something we had—devoted her full effort to us. Especially when she heard we might buy as many as eight place settings of No. 303 (that's the code in the catalog) plus a serving platter and vegetable bowl.

"That," she told us, after calling the factory, "will be here by 3 p.m." It was then 10 a.m.

When she handed us the price list, we both nearly fell into a bin of Quimper china.

For exactly $475 the order would be ours. Ten years ago, we could have brought home a boat load for that price.

We had budgeted just over $100, assuming that when you go to Mecca, the pilgrims profit.

Recovering slightly, we told madame we would go across the square to the sidewalk café and "pense" (study and discuss). That was fine with her

Over café au lait we "pensed and pensed" and decided we could barely afford two place settings, one serving tray and one vegetable bowl for $127.

Voilà! We marched back to Henriot and madame. She understood our poverty and the smaller order would be perfect.

"But too heavy for you to carry home, monsieur. Just feel the weight of one piece. You must send."

How much to "transport?" She figured.

"Forty dollars."

We did an encore of the original swooning act. Outside on the sidewalk, we "pensed" again.

"I'm for giving up the whole thing," my wife said. "We can do better at home. But we should have at least a souvenir purchase."

We scaled down to one serving tray at $35.

Madame looked crestfallen but took it like a good soldier and bit the bullet.

Then, as we were leaving the shop for the time, I said, "But, heck I came to get at the very least two coffee cups and saucers. That's what I really came for."

Back inside the shop. Madame brightened slightly when she heard my additions.

That's what we finally carried out of the shop later that day for just more than $68—one Quimper (HB-Henriot) serving tray, two Henriot styled cups and saucers.

"You use them at breakfast?" she said.

"Use them?" I said. "I'm going to sleep with them next to my pillow."

"C'est la vie (that's life)," she said, waving goodbye. (September 18, 1978.)

Vignette of a Breton Saturday

Locronan, Brittany, France. Just west of Rennes, the village scapes change to an ancient, gray granite look of charming antiquity. The first Celtic crosses and "Crêperie" signs begin to appear. Then you know you have left Normandy and come to the land of the Bretons, with their religious fervor, joie de vivre and individualism.

If the faint strains of the bagpipes seem to sift through the warm faintly misty sunlight, it is a heritage still maintained that belongs not to France, but England and especially the Irish, Scottish and Cornish peoples.

The car rises and falls on the hills and bends to the turns and passes mobile snack stands, selling pommes frites (French fries) et cidre (apple cider of heady content, just short of fiery calvados.)

The highway, broadened by modern engineering, narrows to alley width as you snake through the hamlets and villages on Saturday afternoon, the picturesque Breton houses snug against the street.

In the tiniest crossroads, unable to support even a mini-grocery store, a traveling market van has set up in the village square to save "mère et grandmère" (mother and grandmother) from hopping on their bicycles and pedaling to the next big town to Saturday shop.

This day is market day in Brittany and the large town centers are filled with a pageantry of people and open and covered stands, selling artfully arranged fruits, vegetables— the huge artichokes—fresh meats, Breton pastries, sausages, pâtés, and a variety of household and ready to wear goods. Always looming over all is the cathedral-like church, heart of the minds and souls of the Breton, and often with its singular stone sculpture rising in front.

These are called Calvaire (Calvary) and depict the passion of Christ, plus other scenes from his life. There are modest and elaborate Calvaires and at Pleyben, at midafternoon, we stopped to view the most important in all Brittany, sculpted in the 14th century, now green with age, but amazingly sturdy in appearance, considering the traffic fumes of pollution beginning to spew through the square.

Sitting in the sun, at a sidewalk café across from the Calvaire and sipping a "citron pressé" (lemon squeezed into ice water, with sugar), one is struck by the similarity of all Christian scenes to the Breton landscape.

The stories are all set in Brittany, too.

Because these people are easily persuaded that the Holy Land we know was merely a passing pause and that Christ, his mother and his grandmother—the Virgin Mary and Saint Anne—actually came from Brittany. Or were associated with it.

Thus for the Breton, a trip to the Holy Land, is no further, say, than the village of Locronan, near the Atlantic coast, one of the Breton gems of the past, little changed from the 16th and 17th centuries. The town is a perfect example of the Renaissance, especially the Place, with sloping, uneven granite houses, cobbled streets, mullioned windows and, of course, the church, wherein is buried St. Ronan, patron of the town.

Locronan in the late 20th century is also where we found a new style French country hotel-restaurant, fresh as the daisies lining the circular driveway, yet with a feel of old Brittany, too.

L'hotel au Fer à Cheval (The Horseshoe) is the work of a native of Locronan, M. Main Chipon, who also owns a restaurant by the same name in the village, on one corner of the square in a truly 16th century inn.

But his Hotel au Fer à Cheval rambles across a high hill, about a half-mile into the country, off a windy road. The view is of the Atlantic Ocean to the west and the broad and green valley behind it to the east.

The hotel blends the outdoors with the interior so that huge walls of windows in rooms, dining room and lounge seem to project you into the lawns and gardens.

Shaped like a horseshoe, the rooms are as up to date as everything in next year's car.

Dinners, at 7:30 p.m., are sumptuous in quality if not in multitudinous courses. Who needs more than a huge compote of onion soup, a large artichoke with vinaigrette for dipping and small, but whole pan-fried sole meunière? With a cheese tray or sorbet for dessert?

(September 11, 1978.)

Drink a toast to the Greek god Bacchus

Athens, Greece. At 7 p.m. every day—mid-July through mid-September—Bacchus, the Greek god of wine, is lit up across the marquee at the entrance to the Dafni Wine festival, a bacchanalian night of unbelievable dimension.

From the moment the wrought iron gates swing open until 1 a.m. next day, his convivial countenance beams down upon the hundreds, often thousands, who come to sample the grape and dance, sing and eat—a modern version of Wine, Women and Song because all three are in abundance.

For the entry price, plus an outlay of another dollar for your "wine tasting equipment"—glass and glass jug, properly embossed—you are entitled to engage in the nightly orgy officially called the "sampling of the wines of the Dafni-Athens region."

Unofficially, it means that you can drink as much and as often as you like—free—from the series of eight to 10 barrels strategically located amidst the rolling pine forests, glens, nooks and crannies, all providing grape-arbored outdoor tables and chairs, with three self-service Greek restaurants and one sit-down dining room—indoor and outdoor tables with linen, and black-jacketed waiters.

The wines come in 15 or 20 varieties, from the resiny-white Retsinas through the dry reds, Domesticas (red and white) and into the semi and sweet vintages.

Even though your glass is only shot-sized and you are ostensibly there just to taste before making a decision for your dinner wines, the Dafni Wine Festival is no place for those of little faith or discipline.

But, within that framework of moderation, you can have a pleasant evening as we did, arriving by cab just after opening.

The ride is about five kilometers beyond Athens, and the festival grounds are sandwiched between a huge campground and ruins of a Greek monastery. The vineyards surround all these.

Get there early and the crowds are thinner and less boisterous. We strolled the paths, lined with flowers, tiny brooks and bridges. At each tasting station, we sampled one or two wines, tossing what we didn't drink into the troughs that run under the barrels.

When we found a vintage we liked, we filled a jug with a little and sat and sipped and watched the carnival lights and banners and atmosphere begin to envelop the grounds.

Each dining area provides bands, from rock to bouzouki and jazz and swing. The bands begin to tune up about 8 p.m.

By then, we had not only sampled wines, but also checked out the menus at the various eating places and picked one we thought looked the cleanest, although they were all neat and carefully "policed."

Choices are a gamut of familiar popular Greek foods— stuffed grape leaves, moussaka, roast lamb and sometimes Greek chicken. Then there are always rice and spaghetti, and finally the salads—the seafood-anchovy taramosalata, tuna and shrimp salad (the tuna and shrimp are always pureed, served with sliced eggs and always some slices of those wonderfully juicy, sweet tomatoes).

There are Greek salads and Russian salads and Greek pastries. We chose from this array and the total tab for an entree (chicken, lamb, moussaka) and two salads ran to just under $12. The rolls were awful. Hard cold, blah.

We had each picked our favorite—white Domestica for my wife and a soft, dry red for me. I might say that while there is quantity there is not always quality in the wines.

Retsinas offered were far too resiny—maybe because they weren't chilled. There were no Roditys (roses) because that's not a wine of the Dafni area. The reds were passable to harsh.

But one should not expect Chateau-bottled wines or memorable vintages for $1.75.

By the time we sat down to dine, the festival grounds were filling; tables around us occupied by families, clubs, birthday parties, anniversary celebrations.

At one long table, everybody stood up and toasted the winner or loser or celebrating couple and sang a song. They repeated this ritual a half dozen times until the food began to take hold.

Tour buses pulled up outside the gates, disgorging "See Athens at Night" hordes, who filed into special sections of the main pavilion restaurant, where a floor show was in progress.

Meanwhile near the focus of the ground, people had taken off their shoes and stockings, rolled up their skirts, jeans and trousers and were stomping the juice out of a huge vat of white grapes, in a grape-stomping dance.

Up on the highest terrace, the rock music poured out and strolling Greek singers and musicians serenaded the people bunching around the wine barrels, whose source of supply never was exhausted.

As we watched this shot, we agreed that it could never happen in America. Scenes of the recent Stillwater Lumberjack Days, the Oktoberfests in La Crosse, St. Patrick's Day in St. Paul are too vivid in riotous contrast.

Somehow, everybody—young, middle-aged and old—managed to maintain enough equilibrium and clarity of mind to keep a civilized stance—at least until we left about 11 p.m.

Police patrol constantly, but kindly. We saw some young people who obviously had drunk too much, but they were not loud, nor belligerent. And they were in the minority.

The more sophisticated wine tasters of the world might peer down their noses at such ribaldry and festivity masquerading as a Wine Sampling.

But I have attended some so-called Wine Tastings in the fashionable and elite places of the Twin Cities and France and Germany. And theirs is more a charade of pretense because they gulp and drink as thirstily as the wine "samplers" of Dafni.

And at Dafni there is no shame and no hypocrisy. Wine, in the last analysis, is to be drunk. At Dafni, that's what they do.

The God Bacchus and the winegrowers seem pleased. In fact, I'd swear Bacchus winked as we left.

(September 7, 1979.)

Bretons hold pardon fest

Ste. Anne La Palud, Brittany, France. It was one of life's moving experiences, the kind that sends chills up your spine.

At the foot of the hill, they gave each of us a long, thin candle and a four-sided paper cone that shielded the tiny flame from the wind.

Then we joined the procession of 20,000 tourists, pilgrims, Bretons and visitors up the long grassy hill to the brow, where the Atlantic beach and water stretched into the night below and behind us the moving, flickering bracelet of flickering dots. Like being on a Crusade in the Middle Ages.

It is called a pardon and it was created as a religious carnival-festival 1000 years ago here in Britanny, along with the word.

Pardon me?

We did, the thousands of us. We marched in penance, reciting our transgressions and asking St. Anne, mother of the Blessed Virgin Mary and grandmother of Jesus, to grant us pardons.

We did it in unison, singing:

"Sainte Anne, O bonne mère, toi qui nous implorons, entends notre prière, et benis tes Bretons."

"Sainte Anne, O good mother, to you we implore, hear our prayer and bless your Bretons."

There are other Pardons held throughout the summer in Brittany, but this at Ste. Anne La Palud is second only to the Pardon at Ste. Anne d'Auray.

What we were beginning that last Saturday evening in August was a weekend of festivity, religious and material pleasure.

Coming as it did just hours after the announcement was made that a new pope, John Paul, had been chosen, the Pardon of Ste. Anne La Palud of 1978 will be undoubtedly built into the historic legend.

For it must have been the intercession of the good saint herself that brought both events together.

Or so the four bishops and two monsignors told their worshippers and onlookers who covered the grassy am-phitheater-like hill in front of the church that night.

As I looked out across the tapestry of tiny candle lights weaving into a single cover at the ending of the procession I marveled at the faith of the Bretons, who continue to believe that St. Anne was one of them, of royal birth, taken to Nazareth by the angels, where she gave birth to Mary, the mother of Jesus. And Jesus came to visit his grand-mother there at Ste. Anne La Palud, whereupon a spring gushed forth.

A church was built on the beach and later moved to its present site over the hill.

Thus the background for the 1000th Pardon.

During the most fervent prayers, the bright lights of the carnival just beyond the church in the main street beckoned.

And to them, like moths, flew the celebrants at the end of the first night's religious spectacular.

They would all be back on Sunday for the High Mass and return once more at mid-afternoon for the daylight (Grande Parade), complete with banners, Bretons wearing their native costumes, the women those distinctive, striking headdresses called coiffes.

But in between, blending smoothly, the materialism of the festival was not neglected. Nor was it intended to be.

For like all Europeans, the Bretons have a facility for interlacing pleasure for body and soul.

The incongruity of standing in worship and watching masses of people eating, drinking, playing, whirring around in carnival rides, buying tons of junk not 100 yards away was lost on all but us, I fear.

They have done it thus for a thousand years only what was then a Renaissance Fair has taken on the most modern touches.

Like massive tail-gating on Sunday noons in the hay fields, trimmed into parking lots around the village.

Between High Mass and the afternoon vespers and procession, people set up umbrellas and tables, turned block bales of hay into picnic tables and engaged in an orgy of eating.

All the culinary stops were pulled out wide. No Viking nor Kicks nor Twins game ever saw such spreads of chickens, hams, sausages, salads, crêpes, wines, beers, ciders, pâtés, waffles and pastries.

Or fruits and edible fresh vegetables.

Meanwhile back along the carnival rows of stands, those who preferred to eat as they strolled, or at tables in large tents, could choose from veritable block-long buffets.

The kitchen pride of Brittany was on display for sale and also all the imaginable souvenirs you buy and put away at home and throw away six months later.

There were wine stands and beer stands, cider stands and waffle and pommes frites (French fried potatoes) stands. Stands sold ham, pâté, and sausage sandwiches in long halves of French bread. One man roasted tiny chickens, crusted with herbs of Provence. That tantalizing aroma, wafting across the village, drove people to mass gluttony.

The aura of goodwill reigned undiminished into Sunday evening. Even the people filled with more liquid than religious spirit were jovial as the gendarmes helped them into the paddy wagon for a ride to some nearby bastille.

And as we nosed into the ribbons of traffic exiting down the narrow country roads, courtesy prevailed.

One heard "I beg your pardon" spoken in a multi-lingual refrain that echoed across the Breton hills.

(September 9, 1978.)

The tiny island where Christians came to Europe

Iona Island, the Hebrides. The salt spray spattered the several dozen of us in the open ferry boat as it rode the swells rolling off the Atlantic into Iona Bay.

I peered at the approaching coastline of Iona Island, houses, buildings dotted the land rising from the shore. The

fierce wind and rain of the early morning had subsided and
just as the outline of the little village came clearly into focus
the sun broke through a blue break in the clouds.

Ahead on that tiny dot, the last land between the United
Kingdom and the New World, was the focal point in the
Christian world for the last 14 centuries.

Here, on Iona, in 563 A.D. St. Columba and a handful of
followers landed, a vanguard of Christianity, expatriates
from Ireland.

And in the saint's wake came the stream of Christian
missionaries, who brought their religion through Scotland
to England and Europe in a rising wave.

Here, on Iona, was written the Book of Kells, perhaps
near where I stood not long after the ferry landed us. We
had walked up the tiny road out of the village to the
monastery and abbey of St. Columba, restored and still used
by Christians of all faiths and pilgrimages. Here I stood also
by the cross of St. Martin in almost the same pose that Sir
Kenneth Clarke used in the opening of his magnificent doc-
umentary film, "Civilization."

For here, truly, near an example of one of the most ancient
Celtic crosses, did Christian Civilization begin in Europe.

The sun was warming the damp island now and where
mist and rain had been was only clear blue sky. Those of us
who had ridden the ferry took off our jackets and coats and
basked in the heat.

It had been a small pilgrimage for us to come here, starting at 10 a.m. back in Oban when we boarded the
Caledonia island ferry and cruise ship for the 45 minute sail
to the Island of Mull in the Hebrides.

Then we rode in a coach (bus) the 38 miles across Mull,
one of the last unsullied islands of Europe, inhabited by less

than 1000 people and several thousand sheep. Roads are barely passable and wind through low mountain ranges for another hour to Fionnphort.

From there it is the Iona ferry, little more than a conventional fishing boat, which darts back and forth all day, carrying tourists and pilgrims to and from Iona until at sundown the last buses have come and gone at Fionnphort and those still left on Iona have to stay overnight.

Some do by choice, especially those who are looking for that rare place "away from it all" but still with the amenities of life as provided by two good hotels—the large St. Columba and the smaller Argyll.

We had almost two hours on Iona, most of it spent browsing the Abbey grounds, the old cemetery and the museum where there are relics of the burial effigy stones of kings, chiefs and royal personages during the 13th-15th centuries.

Forty-eight kings of Scotland lie in this little cemetery, including, it is said, Kenneth Macalpine, first king of United Scotland.

Duncan, reputed victim of Macbeth, and Macbeth himself, are listed in records as being buried here, too. But we could not find their markers in the time we had to search this hallowed ground—Scotland's oldest burial place.

As we roamed the abbey itself, we met modern missionaries of many faiths—mostly young people—who live here for short periods, in the monastery, maintaining the grounds and buildings, praying, going to services, doing their own cooking and keeping their own house in rooms that face the bay and the madcap world a quarter of a mile and 15 minutes by ferry away.

Perhaps less than 300 people live on Iona, yet there is a school, post office, general store selling the freshest of groceries, a gift shop and restaurant, where we ate cold salmon mayonnaise and the little waitress was instructed to say that it was "just off the point beyond the pier as recently as this morning."

Survival is tenuous, though, despite all the tourists and Iona Community at the abbey. Whole stretches of the year leave the island enveloped in mist, gales, icy weather and deep boredom. There is nothing much to do if you live here. And there are no more dead kings of Scotland, Shakespearean characters or saints en route.

At 3 p.m. the coach started us back along that path worn by 14 centuries of Christian feet.
(September 14, 1978.)

Magic of Vienna endures in fond memories

Vienna, Austria. When I think of Vienna, I have these dreams:

It is near midnight, and my wife and I are sitting in the Paulus Stube over a late post-opera supper of wurst and dark bread and listening to a musician named Sepp play those sugary Wienerlieder on the accordion.

We are sitting in the Staatsoper House, in the 14th row, cheering our own Leonard Slatkin, who has just conducted a performance of the opera "Turnadot," and the crowds are reluctant to let him leave the stage to return to the Twin Cities for his Sommerfest series.

Two nights later, we have just heard Placido Domingo singing Pagliacci, and after 10 curtain calls, the roaring crowd still won't let him go.

Or it is the Tuesday Waltz Night in Vienna Concert Hall, and the Vienna performing symphony rolls through two hours of Offenbach, Strauss, Lehar, Stolz and Kalman in three-quarter time, and the patriotic crowd claps in thunderous rhythm, then rises in tribute for the "Beautiful Blue Danube" finale.

Because Vienna is a magic city where dreams come true, all of these turned real for us during a late June week.

Suddenly we were really there and walking through a kaleidoscope of scenes.

It is Sunday morning, a chill wind for June whipping gray clouds across the city's old castle and palace towers and we hurry with hundreds—to be in line for the Vienna Choir Boys singing Franz Schubert's Mass in B in the Hofburg Kappelle (Hofburg Palace Chapel).

An hour later, around the corner, we rush to find our seats for the Spanish Riding School's Lippizaner horse performance in the glitter of the great performing palace, a show of grace, beauty and power.

It is a warm, sunny morning, and we eat breakfast in front of the balcony of our little, Viennese style Opernring Hotel, looking at the Staatsoper house across the way. Every night I go out on the balcony and say goodnight to this world landmark, and every morning I greet it with a wave of my buttered crescent roll.

Below, on the Opernring Gasse, is the clip-clop of horse-drawn carriages, taking tourists on nostalgic rides of their own back into the time of Emperor Franz Josef.

Every morning as we leave the hotel, we are greeted with "Gruss Gott" from Frau Susie Riedl, the bouncy, happy owner, who sometimes sits to chat with guests and tell them about her hotel and its 60th year, and how it may not be as ostentatious as the imposing Bristol or Imperial nearby, but "they don't have the view of the opera house and the Ring that mine does." Nor a Frau Riedl to make your life happy.

"Of course," she agrees, "the Vienna you dream about and my Vienna may not be the Vienna other people see. It has its faults and problems, and maybe the glamorous Golden Age is gone, but not in the hearts of those who search for it."

Like ourselves.

We couldn't find it in the Café Mozart, near the opera house, the famed setting for much of the movie "The Third Man" and now closed for remodeling. But it was there on a drizzly night, with cobbles glistening, when we wandered into the Sacher Hotel Stube's snug, red velvet and crystal-chandeliered interior for a late coffee and torte.

There is a hospitality about Vienna that kept surfacing for us.

One of my wife's favorite, but fading, Viennese dishes is a meat stew called Beuschel. But when we mentioned that to the man in charge of Paulus Stube, he said, "They do not serve it so much anymore because it is made of hearts and lungs and kidneys of cattle, but once it was a national dish, and if you come back in two nights, we will have it for you—fresh." We did, and it was Beuschel to remember.

There was the woman cab driver, just a month into her profession, who welcomed us to her city and described her home life in detail and waved at other cab drivers with a cheery smile as she darted in and out of the traffic.

"You can walk down the Karntner Strasse pedestrian mall and not worry that your wallet will be stolen or you will be accosted and robbed as you are in Paris or London and New York," she said. We agreed later.

After-dark Vienna has its younger elements mixing with the older, but the Karntner Strasse Mall is not as boisterous or filled with odd-looking people, noisy youths, or people who look threatening. Vienna crowds at night are more reserved, laid back.

Or were we merely imagining it was like that?

Like Frau Riedl, I prefer to remember the Vienna we saw on a sunny, warm noon, sitting at lunch at a sidewalk café in historic old Landtmann's coffee house across from the city hall, and a pair of wedding parties passed by, the brides and grooms on their way to old St. Stephan's Church in horse drawn cabriolets. And a half dozen diners near us lifting their mugs of beer in a toast.

That's Vienna gemütlichkeit at its best.

Vienna's Schwechat Airport the day we left via Air France for Paris:

Soldiers cradling submachine guns patrolling the corridors and arrival and departure lounges in the grim reality of the real world of hijackings.

But the public address system was playing "Wien, Wien, Nür Du Allein" (Vienna, City of My Dreams) as we left.

That's my Vienna.

(July 26, 1985.)

Edinburgh vignettes: a dog, a thief and a bench

Edinburgh, Scotland. The Scottish people love their dogs, especially the wee Scotties and the feeling is often mutual, which begins a tale about perhaps the most famous of these bouncy, long-haired and usually happy pets—Greyfriar's Bobby.

We walked down George IV Street behind the Royal Mile into Greyfriar's district to find the clues, the details and retrace some of the scenes ourselves.

There is, just opposite Greyfriar's Bobby Tavern and Pub, a tiny statue in what once was a public drinking fountain. This is little Bobby, who was a coal black, Scottie puppy in the early 1850s and belonged to one John Gray, a Lothian shepherd.

The two were inseparable companions and ostensibly frequented the Greyfriar's restaurant of the times.

But alas, in 1858, little Bobby's master died and was buried in Greyfriars Kirk behind the pub, just off George IV Street.

The dog was overwhelmed by grief and refused to leave his master's bier, even as John Gray was buried, Bobby trotted mournfully, tail at halfmast, behind the casket.

And when the grave had been filled, the dog remained in a vigil that lasted days and nights, in rain and wind for 14 years.

No amount of coaxing would stir Bobby away and one morning they found him lying there dead on his master's grave.

The story was passed on down through the decades and the fountain statue was erected, then the American Friends of Bobby inscribed a memorial marker to the faithfulness of a Scottie dog.

Walt Disney made Greyfriar's Bobby known throughout the world with a film of the story and the tourists have been coming since on pilgrimages, especially the dog lovers.

Today, you can see the statue, then walk the path into the Wee Kirk to the place where John Gray and Greyfriar's Bobby are side by side in death as they were in life.

If you step into Greyfriar's Bobby Pub for a tribute toast to these faithful friends, you will likely see at the bar a gentleman or two, with a dog on a leash—direct descendants, perhaps, of Greyfriar's Bobby.

Someone, too, will gladly recite again whatever version is current about the shepherd and his dog.

We walked up George IV Street and stopped to watch motorists slow and wave at Bobby. Then, I did, too, and turned the corner.

DEACON BRODIE—There's something more than passable ham salad, steak pie and a tall glass of Youngers lager to occupy your noon hour at lunch in Deacon Brodie's Tavern on High and Bank streets along the Royal Mile.

For it is the former habitat of a strange personality who inspired Robert Louis Stevenson to create a literary master-piece.

His name was William Brodie, who became deacon of the wrights and masons of Edinburgh. Deacon Brodie was, by day, a pious, wealthy and respected citizen.

At night he turned into a thief, a gambler, dissipated and licentious. Since his trade was making keys, he often turned out duplicates for himself he could use to burglarize shops and homes.

But his avarice and crime caught up with him at last and he was exposed for his nefarious night-time marauding through the city and hanged in 1788 from the city's new gallows near St. Giles Church, a few yards from the tavern, on whose property he had made his home.

Using Deacon Brodie as a model, Stevenson fashioned the pair of literary immortals, "Dr. Jekyll and Mr. Hyde," the epitome of the split personality.

IN MEMORIAM—Edinburghers have a restful custom of providing memorials for kinfolk and friends who have died. Restful, that is, for future generations.

The city's parks are filled with varnished and neatly maintained benches, each with a tiny metal plate indicating in whose memory you are sitting and enjoying a brief break from life's tensions.

The inscriptions are brief, but as original as possible, with such endearments as: "Dedicated in memory of George McIntosh, who spent most of his life in this park instead of working." . . . "In memory of dear husband and father, Thomas Duncan, who often took his family here." . . . "For the Wright whose music made life more pleasant in these gardens."

The benches are cemented into the walks, but their sacredness apparently dissuades vandals from adding their own graffiti. I saw nary a blemish on a bench.
(September 8, 1978.)

Night on Syntagma Square

Athens, Greece. Along about 10:30 p.m., you go over to Syntagma Square and begin watching the people. You also go for the French coffee they serve in the section of the string of sidewalk cafes with the red leatherette section or the black or the brown, but the coffee isn't as good. Nor the passing human drama.

You pick a table about halfway toward the street, where the cabs stop to let out the people and pick them up. And you watch them in procession. People and cabs.

There are the young women backpackers, trudging slowly up the sidewalk, the girl at the rear smoking a cigarette, her blouse a soggy checkered thing.

And behind her, mincing like a mare, a red-headed woman wearing a tight, Turkish towel pantsuit of bright red and tottering on spike heels. She's with a youth, wearing a "Where in Hell is Helena?" T-shirt, jeans and running shoes with holes in the toes.

The cabs come and go. Across the street in the near darkness, the neon flashes in blue and red and amber across the roofs of the King George and Grand Bretagne hotels.

You peer into the night at the King George roof garden restaurant, where they are dining by hurricane lights.

Two rows to the left, four Frenchmen meet, kiss each other on both cheeks and then wander off down the street.

An American man in cut-offs and his wife, in chic dress, hanging on to two youngsters, haggle with the newsstand kiosk vendor over the price of a map of Athens. They wander back into the crowd.

A man and a woman get into a loud argument in Greek, or is it Arabic? Or Russian? She stamps her foot. He grabs her by the elbow and they sit down at one of the tables. A few minutes later, they are in a deep embrace.

The waiter brings your coffee and two glasses of ice water. The coffee is the best here. A big pot of fresh ground and milk. Hot milk. Mostly they want to serve you Greek or Italian Espresso. Not this place. Maybe it's because the name on the awnings says: "Toulouse-Lautrec-Dionysus."

Two overdressed and overweight Greek dowager-types settle into the chairs just ahead.

Want to bet they order Greek pastries with ice cream and cake? Good thing you didn't. Their perfume reeks across the area.

Out of the intersection, blue light twisting, siren wailing, an emergency van sweeps past. Everybody strains to see where it went.

Two James Bond types—they wear coats and ties and carry those square attache cases—plop down at the table next to yours. They whisper. They are students.

Your ears are filled with the babble of the evening—a low hum of languages mixing, blurring. A phrase in German, something in French, over there a word of Spanish and then talking that makes no sense at all.

At the cab stand, two couples are fighting about who is first. The driver sits nonchalantly behind the wheel, finally shifts and drives off, leaving in his wake both couples gaping in disbelief.

The women in Athens may be the best dressed in the world. That's my wife's observation, watching the scene. But the men? Bedraggled, unkempt and from "Oddsville." Too tight pants and too loose shirts, no ties, no haircuts, no shaves, no baths. And they walk beside dazzling women.

But this isn't a Greek spectacle. This is the world passing on the corner of Stadiou and Syntagma Square, at night. They are tired, they are happy, they are looking for hotel rooms that don't exist. They smile, laugh, gabble and gobble like a farmyard full of turkeys.

The elegant tourists, who come out of the plush hotels around the square, look no different, as they savor the scene.

They are from Munich, Bombay, Tokyo, Warsaw, Libya and Salina, Kan., and Upsala, Sweden. They are the actors and actresses and the audience, too, of the drama on Syntagma Square.

Oh, you can see the Acropolis a hundred times and sit in the Olympic Stadium, see a week full of Greek ruins. But if you haven't sat drinking French coffee late at night in Syntagma Square, how can you prove you've been to Athens?

(September 12, 1979.)

Index